Hew Ross of the Chestnut Troop

Sir Hew Dalrymple Ross

Hew Ross of the Chestnut Troop

With the Royal Horse Artillery During the
Peninsular War and at Waterloo

ILLUSTRATED

Memoir of Field-Marshal Sir Hew
Dalrymple Ross, G.C.B.

Hew Dalrymple Ross

With an Appendix by Francis Duncan

LEONAUR

Hew Ross of the Chestnut Troop
With the Royal Horse Artillery During the Peninsular War and at Waterloo
Memoir of Field-Marshal Sir Hew Dalrymple Ross, G.C.B.
by Hew Dalrymple Ross
With an Appendix by Francis Duncan

ILLUSTRATED

FIRST EDITION

Leonaur is an imprint of Oakpast Ltd
Copyright in this form © 2020 Oakpast Ltd

ISBN: 978-1-78282-900-3 (hardcover)
ISBN: 978-1-78282-901-0 (softcover)

http://www.leonaur.com

Publisher's Notes

Contents

Memoir

Field Marshal Sir Hew Dalrymple Ross, G.C.B., third son of Major John Ross, of Balkail, in the county of Galloway, and Jane, daughter of George Buchan, of Leatham in East Lothian, was born on the 5th July, 1779; entered the Royal Military Academy at Woolwich as a cadet in 1793, and obtained his commission in sixteen months, March 6th, 1795, before he had attained the age of sixteen. He was sent in the following year, 1796, to Gibraltar, and returned to England in April, 1797, on appointment to the Horse Artillery. He served with his battery in Ireland, during the Rebellion of 1798, and remained there until 1803, when he was promoted to captain-lieutenant, and appointed adjutant to the 5th Battalion at Woolwich, having been given his choice of an adjutancy, or of a re-appointment to the Horse Artillery.

Earlier in that year an application had been made for his appointment as *aide-de-camp* to General Sir Hew Dalrymple, then commanding in the Channel Islands, but without success. He was again posted to the Horse Artillery, in May, 1806, and in July of that year was promoted to Captain, and appointed to the command of the "A" Battery of the Royal Horse Artillery, which he rendered famous in the history of the Peninsular War as the well-known "Chestnut Troop." This battery was then in Suffolk, under the command of the Earl of Uxbridge, afterwards Marquis of Anglesey.

Upon his lordship's return from the army in Portugal, in 1808, he requested the Earl of Chatham, then Master General of the Ordnance, to place Captain Ross's troop again under his command, and in consequence of this application, it was ordered to embark at Portsmouth in November, 1808, to join Sir John Moore's army in Spain. Being detained by contrary winds, the result of that campaign became known in England before the transports had sailed, and it was disembarked, and marched to Chatham.

In June, 1809, Captain Ross had "the good fortune" (quoting from a statement in his own words), "to be again named for the service of the Peninsula," and embarked with his battery at Ramsgate in that month, landed at Lisbon in July, and after a severe forced march, joined the army of the Duke of Wellington two days after the battle of Talavera.

The details of the embarkation and sailing of his battery are of interest in contrast with the corresponding arrangements carried out under his own orders, fifty-five years afterwards, on the embarkation of the Royal Artillery for the Crimea; when each battery and each division was embarked, in every case, with its full complement of officers and men, horses, carriages, and stores, and the employment of steam power enabled the transports to proceed to their destination almost independently of weather. The following are extracts from a private journal kept during his active service:—

Chatham, June 7th, 1809.—Orders were issued for the embarkation of my troop on the 19th of May (the day on which I returned from Scotland, where I had been on leave for two months), but the transports having to come round from Portsmouth to Ramsgate, we continued in suspense till the morning of the 7th June, when by a letter from General Macleod to Brigade-Major Adye, the troop was ordered to move as soon as possible. The order was received by me at 10 o'clock, and the troop marched for Canterbury at 11, and arrived at the barracks at 5 in the evening.

June 8th.—Marched at 7 a.m. for Ramsgate. Sent Jenkinson (his 2nd Captain) forward to examine the transports, and prepare them for our reception. Arrived at the harbour at 10 a.m., when Jenkinson informed me that he had used every endeavour to find the agent without success. Owing to his absence, the commencement of our embarkation was delayed till past 12 o'clock, a little before which hour he made his appearance. I accompanied him round the ships. They are very good, but as he declared it impossible to stow the ordnance and carriages in the vessels containing the men and horses, I am, much against my inclination, compelled to put them all into the *Blessing,* which had been provided purposely for them.

The other transports are the *Rodney,* in which I am, with M'Donald and Dr. O'Brien; the *Phoenis* (Captain Jenkinson, Belson, and Smith), the *Amphitrite* (Corporal Isherwood), *Jane* (Serjeant Braid), *Ruby* (Serjeant Farquhar), the *Ganges* (Bombardier Ownsworth). The embarkation was completed without accident at 8 o'clock in the evening.

June 11th.—Wet and squally morning. Signal made to get under weigh about mid-day.... When weighing anchor, the agent came past in a boat, and informed me that the *Ganges* was ordered into Portsmouth, to receive more horses; she not being completed in the number she can carry.... I represented to Captain Hamilton the injury it would cause to the service, his permitting the *Ganges* to separate from the convoy, unless he could remove the men and horses belonging to my troop into some of the other transports....

June 14th.—The wind still nearly west. Fresh breeze and squally. Men and horses reported to have been transhipped without injury at daybreak.

June 17th.—The wind directly against us; blowing fresh at west. Beating between Brighton and Beachy Head.

June 19th.—Off the Isle of Wight, with a light breeze to the N.E., at 7 a.m., and the convoy well together. The wind continues baffling all day.

June 20th.—Off Christchurch Bay.

June 23rd.—Wind northerly, and a fine breeze. At 8 a.m., the convoy close round us, and sailing nearly 6 miles an hour.

June 26th.—At daylight, run for the land, with a fair wind, but light breeze;

July 1st.—Anchored in the Tagus.

July 2nd.—Transports ordered to move near to the Naval Arsenal, to get ready to land the troop next morning.

July 3rd.—Land the troop without any accidents whatever.

July 4th.—Commence shoeing, and get ready to march. 5th and 6th occupied in altering forge and completing the shoeing, &c, &c.

July 7th.—All ready to march, but have neither sufficient horses nor can I get mules. Receive an order to take 11 horses from the waggon train, and to receive 6 mules from the commissariat. The horses I procure, but not the mules, and consequently defer marching another day.

MOUNTED OFFICER OF THE
ROYAL HORSE ARTILLERY

OFFICER OF THE ROYAL HORSE ARTILLERY

July 8th, Saturday:—I am informed by the acting commissary-general that no mules can be procured till Monday; I therefore determine to march without them, and request Captain Turner, of the artillery drivers, to bring them up to me. As he purposes joining the army as soon as he can, he will in all probability overtake the troop.

July 9th.—March from Lisbon at 5 o'clock, a.m. About 5 miles from Lisbon, the axle-tree of the forge gives way. Leave the wheeler and a party to repair it; which is done by sending back to the arsenal and bringing up a new axle-tree, which the wheeler secures by strengthening it in the centre with strong plates of iron, ... Reached Villa Franca about 3 o'clock—distance 6 leagues; billeted; not a horse galled.

July 10th.—The first 3 leagues good road; the last 6 very bad—deep sand and very hilly. The horses much fatigued, and many galled.

July 11th and 12th.—Halt at Santarem, to stuff saddles and collars, which from the perspiration are become very hard. . . . Finding it impossible with only two collar-makers to keep the saddles constantly safe, the sweat and dust hardening the panels so much, I ordered the blanket to be carried under the saddle.

July 14th.—Through the awkwardness of a driver, a baggage or store waggon was overset. The leaders were allowed to stop on the pitch of the hill, by which the wheels backed off the end of the bridge, and the waggon turned completely over, but happily without injury to men, horses, carriage, or harness, and in a quarter of an hour it was got up, but with great exertion, for it had fallen into the river at least 14 ft. lower than the bridge

July 15th.—Halt on account of being unable to procure wains, mules, and provisions the previous evening. At 11 at night, the quartermaster brings 9 forage wains and 10 mules to the park from Abrantes. I have been obliged to demand the mules, in consequence of the loss of so many horses, which compels me to drop a store-waggon at this place.

The following extract gives an example of an improvised ambulance:—

July 17th.—Having only one day's forage to carry, I am enabled to put the stores on the mules, and give up the waggon to carry Gunner Roberts and Gunner Harvey (the latter got a severe kick on the knee).

ROYAL ARTILLERY DRIVERS

By nailing corn sacks from side to side of the waggon, a very tolerable conveyance was made for them, and on their arrival, I had the satisfaction to find they had not suffered at all, except pain by the jolting.

July 18th.—Halt. . . . Many horses are far from well, but I hope to be able to take them all forward. Their complaint appears to be rheumatism, brought on by the great heat of the day and damp at night.

July 21st.—Halt by order to forage the three following days. No wains to be procured, which will prevent my marching tomorrow. Wheel repaired and horses shod.

July 22nd.—So much am I reduced in my horses, that I feel it necessary to drop and leave with the commissary, my wheel-carriage and store-waggon. I expect the mules, but cannot build upon them with certainty, otherwise would take the latter forward.

August 2nd.—To Talavera. Received orders to halt my troop on the road, and that the army was to retreat the following morning.

The letters from which the following extracts are taken, were written a few days after his having joined the army:—

To his sister

Gasiesigo,
August 9, 1809.

I marched from Lisbon on the 9th of last month with my troop alone, with orders to join the army as soon as I could. I consequently used all diligence, and though opposed by many difficulties from want of forage and provisions, as well as being deficient in horses, and having the heat of the climate to endure, which at this season is intense, I reached the army at Talavera on the 2nd August, without having suffered one hour of ill health, and left by the road only two men from sickness. You will easily imagine my vexation on finding I was too late to share in the actions of the 27th and 28th—certainly the most splendid in point of gallantry that were ever fought—and my still deeper mortification on learning that we were to commence our retreat the following morning, which we did, and are thus far on our way, it is thought, to Lisbon.

I have now been marching exactly a month, with only one halting day; you may therefore form an estimate of how my time is occupied. In fact, it is a round of eating when we can get it, sleeping when we have time, and working hard almost always. I was only a short part of a day in Talavera, and therefore could not see many of my friends who had the misfortune to be left there

Victor has treated all the prisoners he has taken with the greatest attention and kindness, and has, I am told, assured Sir Arthur by an officer left for the purpose of requesting, that every act of humanity and attention shall be shewn to the sick and wounded. Since we left Talavera, we have performed a wonderful march, and crossed mountains which it is hardly possible to suppose artillery could have been got over. We are now four leagues from Truxillo, to which place I believe we shall march tomorrow, unless it is found necessary to wait for stragglers and the stores to come up. Our arrival here today has given us new life, in the hope of having better food.

For four days we had only one biscuit and half a pound of flour between every six men; now we look for something that may make up for the past, by getting into a more plentiful country. I really believe we should have starved had we continued a week longer in the mountains. How thankful I ought to be for possessing such a constitution. Every one of my officers has at times been ill, from fatigue or climate, but I have not had even a moment's uneasiness. By the march we have made, and the start we have got of the French Army, it is not thought we shall be close followed, particularly as they may be anxious to annihilate the remains of the infamous Spanish Army. The world, it is to be hoped, will now give credit to Sir John Moore's opinion of the state of this country, and I have no doubt will see the rashness of venturing so far as we have done with so small a British force.

My next letter, in all probability, will be from Lisbon, where I have no doubt we are making our way. From what I have said, you must not suppose that this army is at all out of spirits; far from it. They endure every want with the greatest fortitude, and as we have now a prospect of plenty, only lament the necessity there is for our retreat, owing to the unwise policy or cowardice of the Spanish Army. . . . My troop is attached to the cavalry under General Payne, who has shown me every mark of kindness and attention. I may venture to say, what few in the army can, that we have—I mean my troop—been never without some food, though sometimes a little hungry. Jenkinson is an excellent cook, and Hayter a good forager, so that I can never want.

The following letter was written to his aunt, Miss Ross, on the same day:—

I have at last found time to get at my paper and ink; you will have rejoiced at the honour acquired by the British Army, in the actions of the 27th and 28th July, and pitied me for not having had a share in their glory. After a most fatiguing march from Lisbon, we reached Talavera on the 2nd August, just in time to join the cavalry and commence our retreat the following morning. You may judge of our vexation and disappointment when I tell you that, having heard that the army was again to attack; I had marched my troop two forced marches on the two days preceding, in the hope of being up in time—six leagues the one, and eight the other—which, after so long a march as we have performed without a rest, has proved very unlucky; but I have still the satisfaction to see both my men and horses more healthy than the rest of the army, and in better condition.

The want of forage in the mountainous country we have come through, has been a great evil, and we have also been ill off for provisions. For cattle we have had enough, but we seldom see either bread or flour, and when we do, it is but a scanty allowance. The cause of our retreat you will have heard of in England. The story believed here is that Cuesta would not agree to Sir Arthur's wish to attack the French previous to their being reinforced. The consequence was that when they were, from Madrid, the French attacked us. The event you know; it was glorious to the British Army, and will ever be the wonder of every one. Our army only 17,000 men; that of the French 45,000.

As to the Spaniards, they hardly moved in our favour, and the enemy heeded them not. The enemy after the action being, like ourselves, entirely without provisions, retired towards Toledo; and it being ascertained that Soult and Ney were advancing through Placentia—the only route open for our supplies, and through which I came only a few days before—it became necessary to make a desperate effort at our retreat, by crossing the bridge of Archiebispo, which we did on the 4th, and sent immediately to secure the boat bridge at Almaranca, opposite to which Soult, Ney, and Mortier were when we took possession and destroyed it.

We have crossed mountains which, until tried, appeared quite inaccessible to artillery, and which I am informed the French, when they crossed them, did not attempt to carry artillery over. We are now again in a better country, and hope will find a better supply of provisions and forage. It is not known whether we are making the best of our way to Lisbon, or that we are to take up a position at Abrantes. . . The Spaniards have proved General Moore's report to be too true: their armies are plentifully supplied when ours must starve, and they lend us little or no help. They are well pleased to see us fight, but they will not fight for themselves. In short, it is but too evident that we had no business to be where we are; for unless we had an army strong enough to command the Spaniards as well as to beat the French, we can do no good. Our march is the most melancholy scene possible to conceive. The sick and wounded who follow the army to escape being taken, are not to be numbered; and many die by the road side of fatigue or hunger.

As yet, I have been very fortunate in not being an hour ill, and I have only dropt two of my men, who are now in the hands of the enemy, having left them sick at Placentia. It is calculated that there are at least five thousand men left sick in the different towns in Spain, most of them where they can have no medical assistance. At Talavera, we have left a vast number, but they will be well off, as there are many surgeons left with them.

Three days later, 12th August, he writes from Oporto:—

Nothing can exceed the good spirits and pleasing prospects every person I meet here evinces in his looks; but alas! I am just told that the mortifying reverses of the Austrians have turned all our expectations topsy-turvy in an instant. On my arrival, I found the town—which is beautifully situated on the banks of the River Douro—illuminated at all points, and the air re-sounding with the shouts of exultation, and the din of bells and crackers, which uncouthly expressed the joy of the natives for the brilliant victory of Talavera. For a distance of four miles, this animating scene enlivened the banks of the river, as the boats slowly conveyed me from the entrance of the harbour to the town, which I reached when the *fracas* was at its height.

Everything had the appearance of magnificence and prosperity, and even next day I found with great pleasure that Oporto—though the atrocities that Soult's army were guilty of in it cost it many lives—still contained an abundant populace, and that no part of the town had been burnt. The people again recover confidence and exertion. A British officer is appointed Governor of the District, and has roused them to some exertion, and keeps them in some order, which late events had given an opportunity to daring and bad characters to interrupt.

The following extract from a letter to his sister, dated Merida, September 25th, shows how little the brilliant campaigns which were to follow the retreat from Talavera were then expected:—

I have now, I think, given you a good dose of Spain. I have only to add that I shall ever lament the ill fortune which has attended me in the service of this country; to be twice embarked for it, and at last to arrive just too late to witness and share in the most brilliant battle that was ever fought; to have undergone the fag of a long and rapid march up to the enemy, and to have partaken of all the wretchedness of a retreat; and now I only look forward to a lagging march into Portugal, and perhaps some months hence to embark for England, without my troop having occasion to fire a shot, although it has suffered more from fatigue and ill health than in all probability it would have done in many battles.

Much as the climate has disagreed with the men of the army, with the English horses it is still worse.....This brigade (General Fane's) which landed at Lisbon between four and five months ago, 1300 strong in horses, is now reduced to 800, and of that number not above 20 horses have been taken or killed by the enemy. I have likewise lost many in my troop, but luckily my own, like myself, stand the climate quite well; indeed, I never enjoyed better health, nor have I had an hour's illness since in the country.

We have just received an increase to our force, of Captain Bull's troop of Horse Artillery, in which is Ramsay, and the Royal Regiment of Dragoons. They are on their way from Lisbon to join the army.

The troop arrived at Talavera on the 2nd August, and joined in the retreat of the army the following day. To return to the journal:—

Aug. 6th.—To Mesa del Thor. The hills very steep; ten horses to each gun and forty men. Mountainous scenery very fine.

Aug. 7th.—To Campillo. Road very bad, and hills very high; ten horses to each carriage. Here I was obliged to break up my wheel carriage, after taking all the good wheels off it to complete the other carnages, and the next morning, my last baggage waggon being overset and much damaged, I was under the necessity of leaving it, after breaking it up.

Aug. 8th.—To Delcitosa; about two miles from which we quitted the mountains.

Aug. 26th.—March to Merida.

Sept. 2nd.—During the two first days my troop were on this ground, I lost eight horses—that is to say, four dropt down on the march from Medellin, and four died in the lines the following day. Both men and horses continue very unhealthy.

Sept. 20th.—General Fane's Brigade, together with my troop, continued in camp until today, when we move into quarters in the town of Merida.

Sept. 27th.—March to Lobon, where I meet Bull's troop, which is on its way to relieve me at Merida. Dine with him and N. Ramsay.

Sept. 29th.—March to Badajos. Dine with Lord Wellington; forget being in a fortress, and find the gates locked when I wish to return to camp on the other side of the bridge. General Howorth gives me a bed.

Sept. 30th.—Leave my carriages to be repaired in the arsenal, and march with men and horses to Elvas.

Oct. 16th.—Receive a verbal order from General Howorth to leave two 6 prs. with the reserve, as he can give me neither men nor horses.

Oct. 17th.—Form my troop into four subdivisions.

Oct. 18th.—Send Macdonald to Badajos, to bring over two guns and ammunition waggons.

Oct. 19th.—Belson brings the other division from Badajos.

Nov. 1st.—Robe inspected my troop, and expressed himself much satisfied with the improved condition of my horses.

Dec 16th.—March from Elvas to Arronches, where I place myself under the orders of Brigadier-General Robert Crawfurd.

Jan. 12th, 1810.—Receive a letter from Colonel Framingham, informing me that Captain Lefebvre's troop is ordered out to relieve mine, and that after completing Bull's deficiencies, the remainder are to be embarked for England.

Jan. 13th.—Answer Colonel Framingham's letter, and request that he will use his endeavours to induce the Commander of the Forces to detain my troop whilst there exists so early a prospect of active operations.

Jan. 20th.—Receive a very kind letter from Framingham, lamenting that he cannot with propriety counteract the orders of the master-general, by making an application to Lord Wellington to detain my troop. So, all hope is fled.

The battery appears, from the few entries in the journal of this date, to have remained stationary till March. The entry of the 7th March, records:—

Troop inspected by Colonels Framingham and Robe. They express themselves much pleased and surprised at the condition of my horses.

On March 15th, the battery was again on the move, under General Crawfurd's orders.

March 23rd.—Two wheels of the howitzer broke down.

March 25th.—Ordered to give up six of the ten bullock cars attached to my troop; in lieu of which, General Crawfurd has directed the commissary to supply me with a brigade of twelve mules, with a capitross and muleteers. He has also given orders for my being provided with a mule cart, for the conveyance of spare wheels, instead of their being carried on one drawn by bullocks.

April 7th.—Receive a letter from May, telling me in private that it is determined that Lefebvre's troop relieves mine as soon as his horses are sufficiently rested after the voyage.

The next entry on this subject was more satisfactory :—•

May 15th.—Receive a letter from Colonel Framingham, stating that General Howorth had directed my troop to be completed immediately from Lefebvre's, desiring me to send Fisher a return of what I wanted, and him a copy of it. General H. reached head-quarters on the 12th.

The immediate cause of this change in his prospects of service, is explained in a letter to his sister, dated May 20th:—

The French are not yet strong enough to force us out of the Peninsula, and neither of us are at all disposed to quit it till the army does, and that at present does not appear at all probable. I shall have a quarrel with my friend Macdonald for entering into a flirtation and correspondence with my good mother, whenever I meet him, as well as for his giving you such ill-

C. Ortega

Santander

Corunna Ferrol
C. Penas

Oviedo
Valmased

Minho Lugo
Espinosa

Leon
Saldana

Villafranca
R. Esla
Carrion

Vigo
Astorga
Valdaras

R. Sil
Benevente
Valladolid

Villupando
Medina

L
R. Du

Oporto R. Douro
Tordessilas

A
Salananca
Villacastian

Almeida
Ciudad
Rodrigo

Busaco
Fuentes
de Onoro
Guadarama M

40
Coimbra
Aranjuez

G
Talavera

Vimieiro Abrantes
Tagus R.
Toledo Almor

Santarem
S
P
A

Torres Vedras

LISBON
Badajos

P
Medellin
Guadi

O
Albuera

R
Sierra P

Guadiana R.
C.

T
Baylen

U
Cordova

G
Seville Guadalquivir R.

C.
St. Vincent
Malaga

36
Cadiz Barrosa

C. Trafalgar
Gibraltar

8°
4°

F R A N C E

Sebastian
Bayonne
Fuenterrabia
Durango
Roncevalles
Pyrenees Mts.
Vitoria Pampeluna
Calahorra
Figueras
gos
Gerona
Tudelo Ebro R.
Saragossa
Lerida
Barcelona
ro
Mts.
Siguenza
s of Somo Sierra
Tortosa
Tarragona
ADRID
Ucles
40
ana
Majorca
acid I
N
Murviedro
na R.
Valencia
Iuiza
orena
Castalla
s dela
olina
Alicante
Murcia
C. Palos
Cartagena
anada
C. Gata

Map of the
SPANISH CAMPAIGN.

English Miles

0 20 40 60 80 100   200

founded intelligence respecting my troop. Fortune seems to have been willing to make up to us for past disappointments in the ill luck of Captain Lefebvre's troop, which was coming out to take my place; for by the mishap of one of his transports (which was for a time supposed to be lost) losing her masts in the Bay of Biscay, she was driven into a port in Ireland in the utmost distress, having been on fire in this helpless state, and very narrowly escaping shipwreck.

The consequence is that mine being found more effective than his troop, it is ordered to be completed from his. He is also to give to Captain Bull whatever he may require, and with the little that will then remain of his troop, *Lefebvre* instead of *Ross* will proceed to England to make a new troop. I am much afraid that this arrangement will not be so agreeable to you, my dearest Mary, as it is to me and to my friends here with me, who have been at times contemplating with no very pleasing sensations the mortification of quitting this country whilst our army remained behind us.

To return to the journal:—

June 2nd.— . . . . Jenkinson to be at St. Jago on the 5th, to receive the division, &c.

June 15th.—Captain Whinyates and Lieut. Dunne arrive here; the former to see the advance posts, &c., Dunne to do duty with my troop.

June 16th.—The enemy have made considerable advances in their approaches to Rodrigo. Their lines appear in a state of forwardness, and they are constructing mortar batteries—though we do not learn that their artillery are yet arrived. . . Purchase a deserter's horse at auction for sixty-three dollars, and saddle for eleven. An officer ordered to construct a battery for one gun at the ford next above that leading to Carpio. Captain Jenkinson for this duty.

June 17th.—Lieut. Smith ordered to construct a similar battery on this side of the Carpio ford.

June 19th.—Ordered to send an officer to construct a battery for two guns at the hill above Puentecilla.

June 20th.—An officer ordered to the ford of Molines Flores to direct a road to be cleared for artillery, from the Casa del Campo to the height commanding it.

The troop was twice turned out this day, in consequence of a strong reconnaissance by the enemy, and the time of its more active employment was now beginning. The enemy's preparations for the siege of Ciudad Rodrigo are mentioned as "wonderfully advanced."

July 4th.—The enemy attacked the Light Division on this day, and Captain Ross was informed by General Crawfurd that, by the report of many deserters since come in, the fire of the artillery was most destructive.

July 10th.—An unfortunate affair occurred, in which Colonel Talbot, of the 14th Light Dragoons, a quartermaster and 9 men were killed and 9 wounded, and 40 horses of the 14th, the hussars, and the 16th, killed or rendered unserviceable in an attempt to surprise a patrol, which "from daily observation was known not to exceed 30 dragoons and 200 infantry." At the close of the account of this affair given in the journal of this date, Captain Ross concludes a criticism of its management by saying:—"Add to this, the scene of action was a plain, where Horse Artillery could have been used to the greatest advantage, and were not called upon; and that the officers posted in command at the different places were left ignorant of the points from whence they were to look for support."

The next entry is as follows:—

July 12th.—Sent for by the general in the evening, who enquired if I had got my ammunition, and after some time spoke of the affair of yesterday; said it was unfortunate, and appeared desirous of drawing from me my opinion respecting the use that artillery might have been made of, and hinted that he thought they would not. In answer, I remarked, in such an open country we could move with great facility; upon which he dropt the conversation, and desired me to dine with him tomorrow.

The following extract describes the action of the Coa—the first of the many more serious engagements in which Captain Ross and the "Chestnut Troop" took part:—

July 24th, Thursday.—The night extremely wet. March to our alarm posts at daybreak, and all appearing quiet we return to our quarters, when the enemy advance, and we are ordered to meet them. I join the guns on piquet with two more, sending Jenkinson to the right, on the road to Junça, with the 2nd Division. The enemy advance rapidly, and take possession of a commanding height with their cavalry and two guns, from whence they return the fire which we had opened upon them, but without doing us any mischief from this ground. I am ordered to retire by General Crawfurd. We occupy a rocky height in front of the town for some time, but the French kept beyond our reach, sending their riflemen close up to our position, when General Crawfurd directed me to retire upon the town.

About this time the guns under Captain Jenkinson were ordered from the right to join me at the town, and immediately afterwards the enemy's columns of cavalry and infantry advanced upon our right, occupying the ground just vacated. They charge the 95th, and endeavour to cut off the 52nd Regiment, which the skilful conduct of Colonel Barclay alone brought off, together with the piquets of the 95th, and one of the 3rd Cacadores. Finding that his right was completely turned, and that there was every prospect of their getting betwixt him and the bridge, General Crawfurd ordered a retreat. Lieut. Bourchier, of the artillery, brought me the order 'to retire as rapidly as in my power across the bridge, and to get my guns into position on the opposite heights.'

At this time, we had five guns in action, firing upon a heavy column of cavalry moving apparently with the intention of charging us down the Junça road. Our fire was excellent, and broke them two or three times. Upon receiving the order to retire, I instantly sent to desire the quartermaster to move off with the waggons, which were still under the walls of Almeida; for, notwithstanding that I requested General Crawfurd's leave twice during the morning to send them across the river, he would not permit me to do so.

We were singularly fortunate in getting all the carriages across. One waggon was overset, but by the exertions of M'Donald and Bourchier, it was got safe off. During the time we were passing down the hill and up the heights on the other side, the enemy kept up an incessant but ineffectual fire upon us. The cavalry followed the artillery and the infantry, standing their ground wherever they could, and giving us time to get off. It was about nine o'clock when we crossed the bridge. The enemy pursued the infantry close down to it, possessing themselves of every wall as our people fled from it, and persevered in their efforts to force the bridge till three o'clock. They succeeded in getting about thirty men over, but they could get no further; when, concealing themselves behind rocks, they kept up a destructive fire.

They brought four guns to bear upon us, but they could not stand our fire, being obliged to shift their ground without firing more than three rounds in any one position they took up, and at last gave it up altogether, leaving us the power of commanding their infantry without interruption. About half-past four or five o'clock the infantry, together with four of my guns, were ordered to march towards Valverde (where the cavalry had been sent on crossing the bridge), leaving two guns along with the infantry piquets above the bridge. At seven o'clock the piquets are drawn in, and the whole division march to Carnathal, leaving cavalry piquets in front at Valverde. . . . The attacking force, Ney's corps, 24,000 strong.

Captain Ross's brother—a most promising officer of Engineers, who fell at the siege of Ciudad Rodrigo—writes at this date, June 28th, 1810:—

Hew is quite well, and has the magnificent spectacle of a siege to look at. He had just been examining the enemy's batteries and approaches with a glass when he wrote. His general, who is ever active, has converted two of his officers into Engineers, and is going to make battering guns of those of the Horse Artillery.

Again, July 24th, 1810:—

Since I closed my last, I have learnt that the enemy have driven General Crawfurd across the Coa. They advanced in very superior numbers, and I am sorry to say our loss has been considerable. . . . Hew's guns did their duty. He lost only two horses killed and two wounded. His troop is very fit for service, and I hope he will be fortunate. I understand General Crawfurd is rather civil to him.

The battery took part in the Battle of Busaco, on the 27th September of this year, and on the 30th October and 2nd November his brother writes :—

I have been here two or three days with Hew. He is in excellent health. His troop most complete, his horses the admiration of connoisseurs in horse flesh, and officers and men in excellent health. . . . I will venture to assert, and Lord Wellington I am certain could not deny it, that the greatest loss the enemy sustained was by our artillery; and the guns which had the most duty, and I believe I might say that were best placed for effect— even if nothing is said of the admirable manner in which the guns were fought—were those of Hew's troop. . . . Several officers who remained on the field the day after the retreat, amongst others General Crawfurd himself, were convinced more than those who only looked on it from the heights, of the immense slaughter the enemy sustained from the shrapnel shells thrown from my brother's guns, aided for a short time by those of Captain Bull's troop.

Captain Ross himself writes to Sir Hew Dalrymple on the 29th December, 1810:—

Within these few days we have put on a more active appearance. Drouet's corps, consisting of 3,000 cavalry and 12,000 infantry, is approaching Massena. The head of his column, it is said, would reach Thomar yesterday. In consequence of this reinforcement, all the bridges of the Rio Major have been mined, and the necessary precautions for their effectual destruction taken. Measures have also been taken within these two days to have the way clear for a speedy retreat to our position, should they shew any intention of disturbing us in our present cantonments. . . . . Whatever change takes place must be in my favour, for my troop has been so hardly and unfairly worked since here, that any alteration must be for the better. I have the mortification of seeing my troop alternately in the highest health and condition, and the very reverse, through the most absurd misapplication of the service. At present we are stuck as artillery of position on the heights looking towards Santarem, where we are certainly much more for show than use, and where both men and horses have suffered extremely from the exposure to weather, which for some time was very severe.

The next year, 1811, was one of continued active operations, and Captain Ross was present with the Chestnut Troop at the actions of Pombal and Redinha on the 11th and 12th March, Cazal Nova and Foz d'Oronces, 14th and 15th March; Sabugal, 3rd April; Battle of Fuentes d'Onore, 5th May; and the action of Aldea Ponte, 27th September. The distinguished conduct of the battery was noticed by the Duke of Wellington in his despatches of 16th March and 2nd April, and after much delay and difficulty, Captain Ross's services were at length rewarded, on the 31st December, by a grant of brevet rank, and a precedent established for which the corps of Royal Artillery has mainly to thank Captain Bull and himself.

A friend of his brother's writes to him on the 12th March:—

The enemy retired in the night, and we did not overtake them till within three quarters of a league of Redinha. They were posted on heights at the extremity of a heath, having a view of their front of two miles. The country we were marching through was very close and intersected. On their right was a wooded hill. Our Light Division was ordered to drive them out whilst our columns were coming up, which they did in great style. Our columns then deployed into two lines and a reserve—35,000 men—and advanced across the heath, being under a considerable cannonade; our guns as usual in front, and your brother most conspicuous. It was a beautiful sight; every man could be seen at the same time. The enemy could not resist, and were driven down the hills through Redinha, the guns cutting them up famously. Redinha they burnt.

And on the 16th March:—

The enemy is now posted close to the Alva, and I think it probable his lordship will attack them there. Massena has ordered every town and village to be burnt as they quit it, and too faithfully is the order obeyed—scarcely a house escapes. Your brother was grazed by a musquet ball in the right shoulder, in the affair of the 12th, and last evening was struck by a spent ball on the leg, but I am truly happy to say the army will not lose his services by them, he feeling very little inconvenience from either. Your brother is as fine a fellow as ever I saw, and his troop ought to gain him a medal. Nothing was ever better.

The following are extracts from his own letters of this year:—

To his sister

Villa Cortes, Near Celorico,
March 35, 1811.

George tells me he has given you and all my friends at home an account of the busy life we have lately been engaged in, and this must be my excuse for a long silence on my part. This is, in fact, the first day of clear rest or being under cover since the 6th inst., when we marched for Valle. As Lord Wellington's despatches will reach England before this, it is unnecessary for me to enter into any detail of our proceedings, as you will learn from the newspapers all that is worth knowing—*viz.*, that the French are once more out of Portugal, and that we have had the satisfaction of beating them wherever we came up with them, and that this army is about to occupy the same country we left in September last; Napoleon's vain boasts having completely failed, and his army, which so lately was to have driven us into the sea, obliged itself to seek safety from famine or the sword by the most precipitate and persevering retreat. Massena has conducted it admirably well, but his loss must have been very great in men as well as every sort of military equipment.

I have not yet heard what his loss is estimated at by those who have the returns, but I should guess that we have about 1500 prisoners, and certainly his total loss since he commenced his retreat cannot be less than 5000 men; for, besides those killed in action, a vast number have been destroyed by the peasantry, who never spare a Frenchman, so that every straggler is sure to be cut off.

The cruelties of the enemy to them have been shocking beyond description, and I shall not annoy you by attempting to do so. . . . . I have a good deal of regimental duty to attend to previous to moving forward tomorrow, and I know *you* will not be sorry to hear that we have not a chance of again seeing the enemy I should tell you that Lord Wellington has been prevented pressing the enemy harder than he has, by the difficulty he has laboured under of bringing up supplies for the army—everything coming from Lisbon. Could our supplies have kept pace with our capabilities of marching, I really believe we should have annihilated their whole army. As it is, we have given them a lesson, and obliged them to destroy a great proportion of their artillery, artillery carriages, and ammunition.

My troop has had the good fortune to take an active part in all the affairs that have taken place, and I have had the satisfaction to know that its services have been handsomely spoken of. Bull's troop, in which my friend Ramsay is, has also been a good deal employed, and deserves its share of credit. He is quite well, as are all my officers; and as for myself, I am always in the best health when leading a scrambling life and well fed, which has been my case; and Hayter continues to work hard and look as well as ever.

To his brother

Villa Formosa,
April 8, 1811.

As Jenkinson promises to tell Fisher to send you his letters to him,

I shall not plague you and myself by going over the same ground, especially as his descriptions are so accurate and clearly told that I might puzzle, but could not improve upon them. I shall only, therefore, tell you generally, in case you should receive this before his, that we beat the enemy at Sabugal.

The whole brunt of the action fell on the Light Division, and their conduct was as usual admirable. There was a good deal of blundering in the affair, or the fate of the enemy would have been more disastrous; as it was, it has done much credit to the British Army. Our loss has been trifling; not more than 150 killed and wounded—all of the Light Division; the enemy's not less than 1300, including about 150 prisoners.

Two guns of Bull's were so closely engaged, that there was much reason to apprehend for their safety, having for some time only the support of a wing of the 95th and the 43rd Regiment, opposed to four guns within 600 yards, and nearly a whole corps of the French Army, which they maintained till reinforced by the rest of the division, when the enemy were three different times compelled to give way, but returned again; and at last, upon seeing the approach of the Third Division, they retired, leaving a 6-inch howitzer on the ground.

On this occasion we had again an opportunity of doing considerable execution, and, with our usual good fortune, with little or no loss—Bull having only one man wounded slightly, and I only lost one horse, killed in the shafts of the gun, and his companion severely wounded, a cannon shot having passed through both.

Yesterday we invested Almeida, in which the enemy have left a garrison, but of what strength is not yet known. We came up with a column marching out of it of about four battalions, with the cavalry, and Bull had the satisfaction of kicking them all the way to Fort Conception.

My troop was kept in reserve, to watch what might come out of the fortress, with the hussars. We took about ninety prisoners, and a very considerable number are killed and wounded. The most of the latter they got off, as they retired in good order, and were supported as they fell back by fresh troops at Valde la Mula, and had the greater part of the 9th Corps on the opposite side of the Dos Casas stream, and Junot with 7000 or 8000 men at Ciervo. Today we hear they are crossing the Agueda.

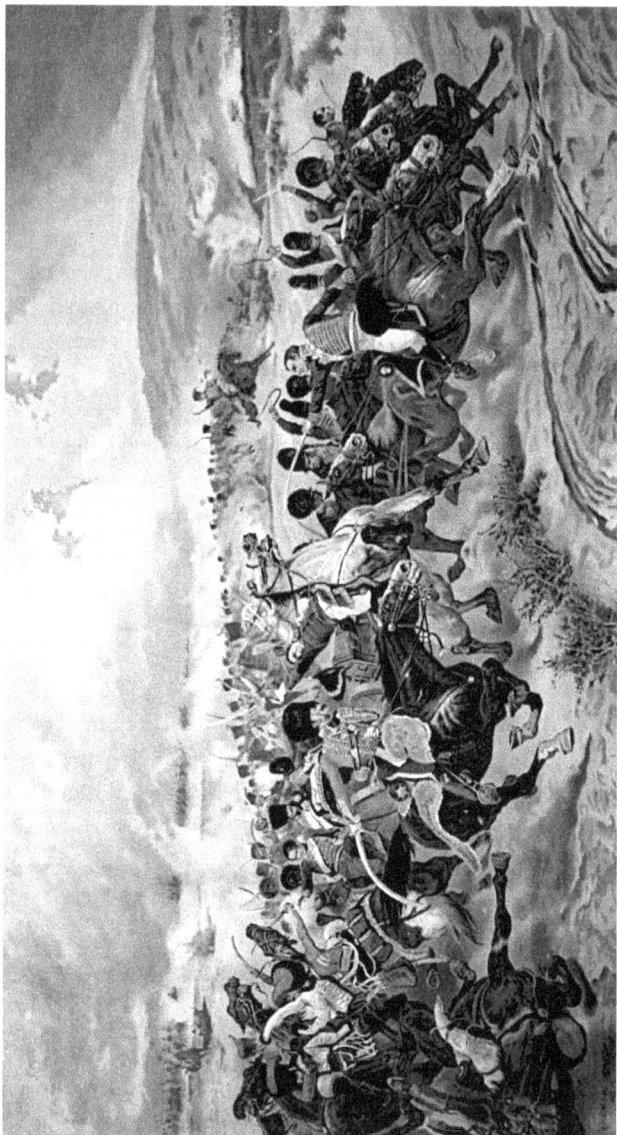

Saving the Guns

Gallegas,

April 14, 1811.

I have a most kind letter from Fanny, as well as one from Sir Hew and Mrs. R——, all of which I have to answer, as well as to tell the good folks at home that I am well, and living in my old *casa*, which I have found exactly as I left it last year, with the exception of the poor old matron, who was about seventy years old, being dead, and the family being not quite so affluent as formerly, owing to the contributions levied by the French. All the Spanish villages, however, are in perfect order, the enemy having done them no harm whatever; and, in truth, I believe the poor people are not over glad to see us back again, as it necessarily makes them look to the chance of war, and the possibility of again changing us for another French Army amongst them. . . . The engineer had proceeded some distance to join this army, when ordered about, and to join Sir William Beresford in the Alentejo. I had a letter from him last night, dated the 5th April, when he was quite well.

To Sir Hew Dalrymple

Gallegas,

April 16, 1811.

I did intend myself the pleasure of writing more fully to you this morning than it will now be in my power to do, as the packet will be made up for England at headquarters this evening, and I am but this instant dismounted at two o'clock, after having spent since two o'clock in the morning in a fruitless attempt to cut off a convoy which was expected to enter Ciudad Rodrigo this morning. This is the third effort that has been made, and perhaps the most ridiculous, having the greatest force employed upon it—the Light and 5th Division, two regiments of cavalry, and two troops of Horse Artillery being moved on the occasion—but unluckily, as on the two former, we found ourselves in the mortifying situation of being just too late, the party having entered the place the preceding night. It is now strongly garrisoned and well supplied.

Not so Almeida, which is expected to fall without the operation of a siege; though it is understood that Lord Wellington, to make sure of it, has ordered the necessary artillery, &c., to be brought up immediately from Oporto; indeed, I believe it is already on the way. In the meantime, he is gone to the army in the Alentejo, having left Villa Formosa yesterday morning, taking the route of Belmonte and Castello Branco, to see how matters are going on there, and to conduct the siege of Badajos himself. He has only taken Murray and Fletcher with him, leaving the other heads of departments at Sir Briant Spencer's headquarters; and I am told he wrote to General Stewart, desiring him to join this army, to which he expects to return in a fortnight.

The following letter to his brother gives a good picture of the incidents occurring at the date of its being written:—

Camp Near Fort Conception,
May 9, 1811.

My dear George,

I received yours of the 21st April last night, and most welcome to me it was, for I grew anxious to hear how you were going on, and must continue to be so until the fate of Badajos is decided, in the proceedings before which place I suppose you will take an active part. Here we have also been leading a life since the 2nd of no common interest. You already know that Lord Wellington returned from Elvas in the utmost haste, on account of Massena having assembled his army at Ciudad Rodrigo, reinforced by everything he could collect in the neighbourhood of Salamanca.

His cavalry is particularly augmented, it is said, by three new regiments, which gives him a very decided superiority over us in this open country. On the 2nd he crossed the Agueda, and on the 3rd advanced with his whole army on the Espeja road, which of course compelled us to fall back from Gallegas to the position intended to be taken up—our right resting upon the heights near Nave de Avea, and our left extending towards Fort Conception, which is occupied by the 38th Regiment.

Upon the 5th, Massena attacked our right with his cavalry, in such force that ours was compelled to fall back after many fruitless attempts to hold their ground. Much gallantry was displayed, but I am sorry to say a great deal of looseness likewise, which favoured the enemy. Our infantry behaved admirably, as did the artillery engaged—Bull, Lawson, and Thompson. I had nothing to say to the affair, being on the left of the whole position.

At the same time that this attack was going on with their cavalry, supported by heavy columns of infantry on the right, the village of Fuentes was hardly fought for. They gained and were beat out of it again no less than five times by the flank companies of the 1st Division—the 42nd, 79th, 71st, and 24th Regiments. The 79th particularly distinguished itself in charging the Imperial Guards through the village in their last attempt.

The enemy left upwards of 500 dead in this village, independent of what might be in the part of it which was given up to them on their side the stream. If you remember the country, it is quite open on our right, which made it prudent to throw back our right flank, which was done by the 7th Division admirably well; the 51st and *Chasseurs Britaniques* received the enemy's charge in excellent style, and beat them back. The right of our position is now at an Atalaja in the rear a little, and to the right of Villa Formosa, and extending from that, through the rocky and enclosed country, down to the Coa in front of Freneda. The enemy occupy the heights and woods on the other side of the Dos Casas. I should have mentioned that he attempted to carry Fuentes on the evening of the 3rd, but was repulsed.

Their cavalry were all drunk, and fought like madmen; but notwithstanding this, and their numbers, 4500 (said to be), they did not do all that they ought. They charged through Bull's guns, who mounted his detachments and sabred a good many of them, and brought his guns off. His loss was trifling. Lawson suffered more severely, both in men and horses, and had a waggon blown up by a shell entering it. After the 5th they remained quiet until yesterday, when nearly the whole of their army was in motion, but with what view I have not heard. It had every appearance of an intended retreat, for they moved off from their left, their columns of cavalry and infantry pointing towards the Espeja and Gallegas roads.

Reignier, however, who is immediately in front of us (the 5th and 6th Divisions), remains without any alteration; and as the country is very woody, Massena may manoeuvre unperceived by us, at least for a time. No doubt, however, Lord Wellington has information from their rear of what he is about. General Pack continues the investment of Almeida, which, I fear, we shall find a more tedious operation than could be wished, situated as the two armies are. If we succeed, which there appears to be no doubt of, the boldness of the undertaking must be the astonishment of the world—a superior enemy in our front, three fortresses invested by us immediately in our rear, as well as a most difficult river, with but one bridge and very few fords over it.

During the night of the 7th, we entrenched the right of our position from Fuentes to the Atalaja I before mentioned, and threw up batteries for the artillery, which secured us from any impression being made by their cavalry, which evidently appears to have been the expectation of Massena. Our loss on the 3rd and 5th is 1600 killed, wounded, and prisoners; amongst the latter is Colonel Hill's company of the Guards, a company of the 71st, and one of the 79th. The enemy's loss has been much greater, but not certainly known. The peasants say 5000, and the prisoners acknowledge it to have been very great. In our army I think it is generally supposed about 3000, but it is quite impossible to form a true opinion on the subject.

As you may suppose, we have been a good deal harassed for these some days past, but we are all in good health, and make no doubt of making an example of the rogues if they dare to attack us. We have been well supplied with everything, and consequently in rare spirits.

Jenkinson desires kind regards to you, and continues to desire Fisher to forward his bulletins to you. Say if you receive them.

To Sir Hew Dalrymple

La Sameida
May 13, 1811

Massena made an effort to restore the spirit of his army, after recruiting it at Salamanca, by assembling every man he could lay hold of, and advanced for the avowed purpose of relieving Almeida, and driving us across the Coa. On the 2nd he had his whole force assembled at Rodrigo, and advanced on the 3rd. We fell back to the position behind the Dos Casas River, and in the evening of that day the village of Fuentes was sharply contested for, but after three attacks remained in our possession.

At six on the morning of the 5th, he commenced the attack with his cavalry, in the open country upon our right, which compelled Lord Wellington to throw back his right from the heights near Nave de Avea towards Freneda upon the Coa. Their great superiority in cavalry made this movement necessary; notwithstanding which, the steady conduct of our infantry and the galling fire of our artillery enabled it to be done without their being able to make any impression.

Whilst this was going on upon the right, the village of Fuentes was five times carried by the enemy, and as often were they beat out of it at the point of the bayonet; and at five o'clock in the evening the action ended, leaving us in possession of our position, they having lost upwards of 3000 men, and our loss being 1700. They left upwards of 500 bodies in Fuentes. On the following days, Massena manoeuvred in our front, favoured by the thick woods his army occupied, and till the 10th it seemed doubtful whether or not he intended risking another attempt. It was then, however, discovered that he was retiring, which he effected in good order, being covered by his numerous cavalry, consisting of not less than 4000, whereas ours was not more in the field than 1000, and, as might be expected, did little or nothing.

Their whole army recrossed the Agueda that evening, and has since marched for Salamanca, Toro, &c., leaving a strong force of cavalry and the garrison of Rodrigo upon the Agueda. In the midst of all this good fortune which has attended this army, we have to lament a sad blunder committed by the troops employed in the investment of Almeida. General Brennier (the governor), finding all hope of relief fled, charged and set fire to his mines, having previously marched out his garrison at one o'clock in the morning of the 11th, directed the march of his column upon Barba del Puerco, avoiding the villages in the way; and so bad was our look out, that, having passed the piquet, but for the explosion he would in all probability have completed his purpose.

It, however, was such as to excite alarm and consequent pursuit, in which 1 colonel, 14 officers, and 200 men were taken and about 300 killed. Where the fault lies, I have not distinctly heard, but it is certain great blame attaches to someone; for a regiment, to my knowledge, was named to march to Barba del Puerco the preceding evening, but whether or not the order was conveyed to it, I know not. It is said that the matter will be the subject of a serious enquiry.

In the place is left an immense quantity of artillery carriages, stores, and ammunition, and a great quantity is destroyed by the mines having been so formed that the wall and revetment is thrown into the ditch, in which is placed carriages and every description of stores. The 7th Division marched yesterday for the Alentejo, and this morning the 3rd commenced its route for the same destination, whither Lord Wellington follows in a few days. As everything promises to be quiet here, I am desirous of getting my troop removed to that army, but I am very doubtful of my success.

The next letter to Sir Hew Dalrymple gives an account of the movements to the date of August 12th, and ends with a reference to his and Captain Bull's failures to procure brevet promotion in recognition of their services:

> Sango, Right Bank of the Agueda,
> and Four Leagues from Ciudad Rodrigo,
> August 12, 1811.

Before you receive this, you will already have heard of our sudden and unexpected move from the south. We were all completely quizzed, having fancied ourselves at rest in cantonments for at least a month or six weeks, and were making arrangements for refit, &c., public and private, when on the fourth day of our enjoyment we received our route. To prove how little it was expected, and how secret Lord Wellington has been of late, I must mention that General Crawfurd had begun laying in supplies of forage and provisions (for upwards of a month to come) for his division, and had even, in his confidence of remaining at Castello de Vide to enjoy it, formed a Division Hospital (which is expressly contrary to general orders), instead of sending his sick to the General Hospital in the rear, by which, when we marched, he left no less than 107 sick to be moved; to transport which he was obliged to send away his provision mules, which have not yet joined, and we have in consequence been very ill supplied during our march—frequently without bread, when the rest of the army had plenty.

Report says that Lord Wellington has strongly expressed his displeasure at this circumstance, but I really believe he has got off much easier than his lordship would have allowed any other officer in his army to escape. Throughout the whole march the same secrecy has prevailed. Generals of division have never known their destination farther than the daily route pointed out, and even the commanding officer of artillery has been kept in ignorance as to the points where he should order his stores for the supply of the brigades in the field to move to.

All this, together with a report that the battering artillery (which was brought from Lisbon to Oporto when we advanced to this part of the country some months ago), with two companies of artillery, are approaching Almeida from Oporto, has led to the belief that we are certainly about to try our luck in another siege.

This idea may also be strengthened by the circumstance of Lord Wellington having fixed his headquarters at Guinaldo, and by his having yesterday reconnoitred the *Sierra* and the passes through it. He slept here the night before (having Generals Graham, Stewart, and Murray, and two of his *aides-de-camp* with him), leaving the mob and baggage at headquarters.

He set off at four in the morning, passing through the mountains, and was to go to St. Espiritus on the Salamanca road, and from thence return by San Felices el Chico, and cross the Agueda below Rodrigo to Gallegas before night. Today he is again at Guinaldo, and I am told

The Duke of Wellington passing the R.H.A. on the march

we are likely to be a few days at rest before anything is undertaken. The Light Division and a squadron or two of cavalry only are on this side the Agueda, and they were employed in blocking Rodrigo during the reconnaissance. We approached as close to the place as their guns would permit, but they shewed only one field gun and a few infantry outside the walls.

The garrison is said to consist of not more than 1500 or 1600 men, and I could not discover any other alteration since their possession of it than their having occupied the height from whence they made their attack with a work, but apparently it is not of any very great strength. I should observe that Lord Wellington's reconnaissance of yesterday has more the appearance of his wish to gain a knowledge of the country upon which he might have to fight a battle to cover the besiegers, than a further advance, which some think he will do in the hope of destroying the enemy's magazines at Salamanca. It would certainly be a great effort, but I must think that Marmont is too good an officer to allow it to, be effected.

Whatever may be the result, our move to the north certainly promises to be a most important one, for Soult most assuredly cannot allow Rodrigo to fall, and to rescue it, he must give up offensive operations in the south, which we know he is carrying on against the few remaining fortresses in the possession of the Spaniards. I understand that the whole of our force has crossed the Tagus, and moving this way, except the 2nd Division, British; General Hamilton's Division of Portuguese; and two brigades of cavalry—one English, the other Portuguese. They remain under General Hill, who I should imagine will manoeuvre so as to join us should Soult abandon the south and follow Marmont, who is said to have broken up from Placentia and that country, and to be on his march northwards.

I have endeavoured to give you, as far as my knowledge goes, the situation of the army, but I must leave it to you to form your own opinion as to the probable views of our commander-in-chief for the further prosecution of the campaign. The only thing that appears clear to me is that it is his utmost wish to draw the enemy's chief force to the north; but whether or not he will undertake the siege of Rodrigo to bring this about, or content himself with the threat he is making, seems doubtful.

In answer to your question respecting Bull and myself getting rank, I am sorry to own that I am really without any hope whatever, and my despondence chiefly arises from the unmanly and miserable feelings of our own corps. There has ever been a prejudice in the heads of the regiment against inferior officers obtaining brevet, and neither Bull nor myself have weight enough in it to get the better of sentiments so rooted in them. I am told that the packet is making up for headquarters, otherwise I should now communicate what has passed between us and Lord Wellington on the subject through the means of General Stewart (adjutant-general), but I shall do so next week.

His answer to our statement was civil, and put the question from himself. Every captain promoted was junior to us, and in the light division I have had the mortification of seeing many step over me with whom I have been constantly present during every service they have been in during the campaigns in this country, for which it is declared that they receive the reward and honour of promotion. This is a subject which I should never have plagued you with, but as you have so kindly led to it, I shall take an early opportunity of putting you in possession of what our feelings are where both our honour as individuals and as members of a corps are so much concerned.

The following is the promised letter, giving a detailed account of the steps which Captain Ross and Captain Bull had taken on the subject of their promotion:—

Las Agallas,
August 31, 1811.

My dear Sir,

In the haste with which I was obliged to close my letter of the 12th, I had only time to threaten you with a tiresome detail of the reasons why Bull and myself consider our prospect of sharing in the brevet promotions recently given in this army altogether desperate. This, as well as other artillery grievances, are subjects which I could willingly refrain from troubling you about, because I have the mortifying conviction of their being quite incurable; but I feel that I should be much to blame was I not more than anxious to show you that we have done what became us in claiming justice to ourselves, and to establish the just pretensions of our corps, and, in short, to put you in possession of the particulars of our case, in which you have taken so kind an interest. I shall therefore proceed to relate them.

About the middle of May, it became the topic of general conversation that Lord Wellington had been instructed from home to send in recommendations for the brevet promotion of such officers as he might think, from their zeal and services in this country, to be deserving of such a mark of the prince regent's approbation, and that he intended in a particular manner to make his selection from the Light Division in consequence of the unremitted exertion it had undergone. This subject was introduced at General Stewart's, when Downman was dining there; and upon the services of the Horse Artillery being mentioned, he expressed a hope that, as Bull and myself had always been acting with the light division and cavalry, if anything of the sort should take place, we might not be left out.

The general immediately observed that he considered that impossible; but, at all events, to prevent our being overlooked, he would have great pleasure in mentioning our names to the commander of the forces, and desired Downman to give him a memorandum, that it might not be delayed through any forgetfulness on his part. Enclosed are copies of the letters that passed. To comment upon the official answer directed by his lordship is unnecessary, neither shall I dwell upon the disappointment it occasioned us. We endeavoured to reconcile ourselves to our fortune, and only hoped to see honours and rewards given to those possessing better claims.

It would not be easy for me to express our surprise when the *Gazette* appeared (we saw and felt our mortifying situation in belonging to a corps which is forbid to hope). In it there was not an individual promoted to major within one year of our standing as captains—some not within three, four, or five years, and I verily believe most of them little more than half our standing in the army.

I trust I shall not justly be accused of assuming more than I ought, when I assert that we possess as much zeal as any of them; that our exertions must necessarily have been greater, from the nature and extent of our commands; that we have shared in all and every service that they have been engaged in; and that the conduct of our corps has in no instance fallen short of any merit that those to which they belong may lay claim to.

I regret that I cannot send you the copy of a letter we addressed to General Stewart upon seeing the *Gazette*, as it is in the possession of Bull, and he is at Alfayates. In it we endeavoured to express ourselves in such a manner as to avoid giving offence to the commander of the forces, but, at the same time, shewing that we strongly felt the injustice with which we have been treated, and hoping that he would re-consider our case. General Stewart, in acknowledging the receipt, assured us he would take the earliest opportunity of laying it before his lordship, which I am sure he would do, but we have heard nothing since on the subject, and have ceased to expect it.

As it may excite your surprise that we did not receive any support from, or make any application through, our own commanding officer, it may be right that I explain that the terms upon which Lord Wellington has long carried on duty with General Howorth, independent of the direct, unjust, and cruel insult offered to him and the corps by the total neglect of their distinguished services at Fuentes, rendered such a step on our part impossible. Indeed, General Howorth would not demand an explanation wherein the honour and character of his regiment was so much concerned, but contented himself with sending a report of the case to the master-general. We could not, therefore, expect him to exert himself for the interest of individuals. Upon his going to England, however, he offered to present any memorial to Lord Mulgrave we might wish, and recommended our sending one; but we have contented ourselves with transmitting him the correspondence that has taken place, with a comparative statement of our services and those captains lately promoted to majors, which we have requested him to lay before his lordship; but for myself, I must own I don't entertain the least hope.

I fear we are far behind our sister corps in overcoming old prejudices in it. They have lately taken advantage of the opportunities offered, to establish precedents which cannot fail to be of the utmost service to them, whilst our senior officers having grown grey themselves in the subaltern ranks, cannot endure the thoughts of their followers being more fortunate, instead of considering it an advantage to their corps that individuals should have the stimulus of brevet promotion held out to them in common with the rest of the army. They reckon upon what they absurdly call the hardship suffered by others whose service may not put them in the way of obtaining it, and cry out against it as an unjust innovation. Of this class I have but too much reason to believe is ——, and to this feeling I attribute his manner of getting rid of the subject when conversing with you.

From this you will be able to estimate the little chance we have through the efforts of our corps; and I have been told by friends of Lord Wellington that he has declared that he never will recommend an officer of either artillery or Engineers for promotion, in consequence of the opposition he met with in his wish to procure a majority for Chapman, and thus, in my opinion, all hope is ended; for though I have heard that the prince has particularly noticed that the artillery had not shared in the brevet, and spoke of it as extraordinary, still the time is past for anything good to arise out of it; and, notwithstanding I am sure —— would do anything in his power to forward both Bull and myself, still it would be too much to expect him to oppose what is too evidently the sentiments of the heads of the regiment.

The situation to which the prospects of an artillery officer are reduced are too melancholy to think of. I will instance my own case (one of the most fortunate in the regiment). After nearly seventeen years' service, I find myself seventy steps from a majority—a ladder which I shall in all probability be at least as many more in climbing, and I am refused a participation in the honour of brevet promotion with the rest of the army when equal pretensions can be brought forward, I must believe, purely because I belong to that particular service. No less than three junior captains in the division in which I am, got the brevet of majors in the late promotions; and though I may allow them a great superiority of merit over myself, yet I must think that the difference of five or six years' service ought to bring my claims pretty near their standard.

I fear, my dear Sir, I have long since tired you with this long story, and I ought also to apologise for the manner in which it is written; but I have been obliged to scribble on my knee, in consequence of having slightly sprained my ankle by a fall from my horse, which has compelled me to lay up for a few days.

I should have mentioned that, in addition to the claims that Bull and myself made upon Lord Wellington for a participation in the promotion, he was also spoken to on the subject by Sir William Erskine, who told me that he spoke in very handsome terms of both, but lamented that it was not in his power to do anything for us, which is quite conclusive in my mind that whilst on this service we have nothing to hope for.

The following are the enclosures referred to:—

From Major Downman to General Stewart.

My dear General,

In consequence of the conversation which passed between us the other day respecting the promotion likely to take place in the Light Division, and your wish that I should write to you on the subject, it appeared to me best that the services of Captains Bull and Ross should be clearly stated, that you might have it in your power to answer any questions as to the merits of those officers which the commander-in-chief might require as soon as the question is agitated.

Captains Bull and Ross, of the Horse Artillery, have served with the Light Division and cavalry both on the late retreat and advance of the army, and, from their separate commands, have held responsible situations. They are the senior officers of their rank in that division, and have also been the senior officers of their own corps in the field during the whole campaigns since August, 1809, and are now near seventeen years in the service.

Captain Bull's services are seven years as lieutenant, four of which were on active service in the West Indies. On the evacuation of St. Domingo, he was fortunate enough to receive the thanks of the commander-in-chief for his conduct in the Grand Lune, and to be recommended by his own commanding officer to England for the same. Nine years and a half as captain of Horse Artillery, two of which have been in this country; and, during the late retreat, has had the satisfaction of receiving the thanks of Sir T. Cotton in public orders.

Captain Ross's services are eight years and a half as lieutenant, one year and a half of which was in the garrison of Gibraltar, and seven years as lieutenant of Horse Artillery, five of which were in Ireland, and during the disturbances there. Eight years as captain, six of which have been in the Horse Artillery, two in this country; during which time he has always been attached to and shared in any services in which the Light Division have been engaged.

(Signed)   T. Downman.

From General Stewart. A. G. O.

Headquarters, Elvas,
May 29, 1811.

Sir,

I have not failed to lay your letter of the 17th inst. before the commander of the forces, and I am directed by his lordship to observe that the promotion to which he was directed to recommend was not to be confined solely to the Light Division, but the selection was to be made from the army generally.

His Excellency took a larger proportion from the Light Division for their eminent services, and he is fully aware of the services that have been performed by Captains Bull and Ross. But their seniority in the army, compared with many officers in this country, cannot fairly at present bring them forward.

I trust, therefore, that the knowledge of the commander of the forces' good opinion of the zeal and abilities which the above officers have displayed will be as fully gratifying to them as if his Excellency had more power to recompense their several merits.

I have the honour to be,
Sir, &c, &c,
(Signed)   Charles Stewart,
M.G. and A.G.

To Major Downman,
Commanding Royal Horse Artillery.

To Sir Hew Dalrymple.

Casillas de Flores, near Guinaldo,
October 8, 1811.

My dear Sir,

Since I last had the pleasure of writing to you, the Duke of Ragusa has paid us a visit, thrown in abundant supplies into Ciudad Rodrigo, and gone back with his whole army to his former cantonments, Placentia, Talavera, &c, as well as sent all the troops he borrowed from the north for the occasion back beyond Salamanca.

Lord Wellington's official despatch will no doubt fully detail the few days' active operations which Marmont's advance gave rise to; I shall not therefore enter into the particulars. The general plan his lordship appeared to have in view has been answered, I should think, to the full extent, in forcing the enemy to assemble (to their great inconvenience) an immense army to relieve the place; and it has also afforded another occasion of proving the valour and discipline of the British troops.

If the Commander of the Forces has been as liberal in his public report as he has been just in his general orders to the individual corps engaged with the enemy on the 25th, it would be fruitless to enumerate them, as you must be already informed upon the subject; but I cannot help mentioning, with real satisfaction, that our dragoons (who it has been the fashion to cry down) did not allow the opportunity to escape them of proving their wonderful superiority over the enemy. The Light Division and my troop have had no share in the fighting, though we had our portion of fag and anxiety.

During the whole of the 25th and until late on the following day, we were completely separated from the army, being advanced as far as the Vadillo on the right bank of the Agueda. When Lord Wellington, with the 3rd Division, had been obliged to fall back to Guinaldo, so doubtful did Crawfurd think his being able to unite his division to the army at one time, that he had absolutely made his arrangements for taking to the mountains, and had given me instructions in the event of such a measure becoming necessary.

Marmont, however, was not prepared to take advantage of our situation; for it appeared that he had only crossed the Agueda for the purpose of making a reconnaissance, but finding only one division (and that dispersed) and a few cavalry in the open country from Pastores to Guinaldo, he pushed on, and but for the admirable gallantry and steadiness of this little corps, there can be no question that he would have taken or cut them to pieces, which would also have involved us in a scrape.

Lord Wellington may certainly place this to the account of his good fortune and the good conduct of his troops; for he was under the most perfect persuasion that the enemy would not advance, and so far, he was right, for it was temptation alone that brought them on. As it was, however, he had a most lucky escape. In the evening of the 25th he was joined by the 4th Division, in no very advantageous position, in front of Guinaldo, and by the Light Division in the afternoon of the 26th, after crossing by the ford of Cagaloços, near Penaparda. The enemy had been bringing up his troops during the whole of this day, and before night had nearly 50,000 infantry immediately in our front prepared for and hoping we would wait for his attack the following morning, for which purpose he actually marched his columns before light on the 27th.

We commenced our retreat at ten at night, and nothing of importance took place, if I except an affair at Aldea Ponte with part of the 4th Division and some sharp skirmishing between the cavalry, and a trifling cannonade occasionally, and chiefly at a distance.

George has been moving with the 1st Division, and is now with it behind the Coa. I heard from him yesterday; he was well. As far as I can learn, the distribution of the army is at present nearly as follows:—

Headquarters, Freneda; Light Division, Guinaldo; 3rd, Aldea Ponte and neighbouring villages; the 4th, Nava d'Aver, Fuentes d'Onor, and Almeida; the 1st, Regiosa, Castanhina, &c.; the 6th, upon the left of the 1st, both behind the Coa; the 5th are at Guarda, and the 7th, I believe, are in the direction of Castello Branco, perhaps Caria, or thereabouts. The cavalry are scattered everywhere, trying to exist, which is almost more than I can say of my establishment.

For the first time since the retreat from Talavera, I have reason to fear that my cattle will be starved and lose condition, every description of forage in this neighbourhood being entirely consumed. By holding this country, two advantages are gained— we are drawing considerable supplies (when the commissariat have ready money) from Spain, and are well situated to oppose any operation the enemy may direct against any part of the frontier, besides leaving Portugal a little quiet.

We are now nearly a month without tidings from England, which is the occasion of much speculation as to public, and anxiety for private intelligence. . . . Fanshawe writes me he is hard at work at Chatham. I hope they are works that will never be called upon for defence; for if they should, independent of other considerations, they would require half the army of England to man them. Adolphus' Colonel, Major-General Vandeleur, has just joined this division; he has succeeded to poor Drummond's Brigade. The major has a fair promise of a step by it, for it is considered a fatal brigade. Barclay, Wynch, and Drummond have all fallen whilst in command of it, and in a very short time after each other.

The next are extracts of the same date (October 8), from a letter to his sister:—

Norman Ramsay promised me he would tell you *all* (through his sister), that as usual I continue in rude health, and had not a chance of getting my head broken in the late scramble. The Light Division and my troop were quite out of the fun, though we were put in for a great deal of fag and annoyance. It has gone near to knock up my friend Jenkinson, who I have been obliged to send to the rear for change of air. He is, I am happy to say, getting better, and I hope will soon rejoin me. You may tell Ramsay's friends when you see them, that he never looked better than when I met him a few days ago. He is now gone with his troop into Portugal, and I have not much chance of seeing him again for some time to come

The enemy having thrown in supplies to Ciudad Rodrigo, have again retired to their former stations, after having got another lesson to respect the British Army, however inferior in numbers. Part of the 3rd Division and a few of our cavalry had an opportunity of distinguishing themselves in an extraordinary manner against incalculable odds.

Major Gordon, one of Lord Wellington's A.D.C.'s, was sent to Marmont with a flag of truce after the affair of the 25th, and as his intended operations were not completed, he detained him till the 27th. Whilst with the Duke of Ragusa, Gordon was treated with the most liberal attention. Nothing could exceed the encomiums passed by him and his staff, as well as every other officer he conversed with, upon the conduct of the British Army.

The claim of artillery officers to brevet promotion having been at last recognised, Captain Ross was gazetted on the 31st December, 1811, to the rank of brevet major, for his services in the preceding campaign. How well the rank had been earned may be seen by referring to the actions in which he had been engaged in that and the preceding year:—Action of the Coa, 24th July, 1810; Battle of Busaco, 27th September, 1810; actions of Pombal and Redinha, 11th and 12th March, 1811; Sabugal, 3rd April; Fuentes d'Onor, 5th May; action of Aldea de Ponte, 27th September.

His services of the year 1812 commenced with the siege of Ciudad Rodrigo, at which he had to mourn the loss of his last surviving brother, who was killed at the assault of the place.

★★★★★★

Of his three other brothers, the eldest, a clergyman of the Church of England, was lost in a ship which was supposed to have foundered in the West Indies. The second died in London. The youngest died of yellow fever while serving as a midshipman in the West Indies.

★★★★★★

His first letter to Sir Hew Dalrymple, after its fall, after alluding to his loss of his brother, proceeds:—

El Bodon,
January 29, 1812.

The official accounts of the fall of Ciudad Rodrigo, with all the circumstances attending it, must have long since reached you. It is, therefore, unnecessary for me to say anything on that subject, beyond stating that I understand the breaches are thoroughly repaired, and two outworks which are constructing (one on the right of that the enemy had, and the other between it and the fortress), are in a great state of forwardness. At present the 5th Division occupy the place, and assist in the arrangements for its defence; but a special garrison from Castanos' army are to be put into it under a Spanish governor, as soon as it is in every respect ready to be given over to them.

In it was found an ample store of ammunition and every other requisite for its supply, together with what is said to have been Massena's battering train, with all its accompaniments of timber, &c, &c, a great part of which not being wanted in Rodrigo, is now moving with every exertion to Almeida; and I am concerned to add that my unfortunate troop is likely to be sacrificed in the performance of that labour, nearly half my horses being constantly employed upon it, and, at the same time, very ill fed.

A few days past we were ordered to be supplied with three days' provisions, in consequence of Marmont's return to this part of the country, and having assembled some force at Salamanca. It would appear that he had not till then any certain intelligence of our proceedings in his absence, and came expressly for the purpose of throwing supplies into Rodrigo. 3000 men advanced to Tamanes, and it is even said he had the convoy ready to bring up, when he learnt that he would not only have the whole British Army to contend with, but that the place itself was in our hands. He of course fell back, having only brought four divisions of his army with him from the south, with which he could not meet Lord Wellington with any hope of success.

The battering artillery has already been put in motion, and to judge from appearance, we shall very shortly make another attempt upon Badajos. Yesterday the iron mortars and howitzers (brought up, but not used against Rodrigo) were to commence their march from Almeida for the Tagus by the route of Villa Velha; and the 24 and 18-prs. (thirty-six in number) have got under weigh some days for Lamego, to be embarked on the Douro on their way to Lisbon.

The next letters are from before Badajos, where Major Ross was dangerously wounded on the forehead at the assault on the night of the 6th April. He had also been slightly wounded in the shoulder at Redinha on the 12th March, and in the leg at Foz d'Oronces on the 15th March of the previous year.

The two first letters were written during the siege; the third when it was over.

To Sir Hew Dalrymple.

Camp before Badajos,
March 19, 1812:

My dear Sir,

I am just informed that there will be an opportunity of sending letters for the English post this evening, which I am happy to avail myself of, that I may acquaint you that we are fairly embarked in another siege of Badajos, which I trust will be more successful than on the two former occasions. The 3rd and 4th Divisions invested the place. On the 16th, and we (the Light Division) joined them on the 17th, and broke ground against the Picurina fort the same night within 300 yards of it. The enemy appeared to be so jealous of the point of our former attack, that, favoured by a very dark and tempestuous night, the first parallels were nearly completed without their having observed our attack, and already a battery for eight guns is in a state of great forwardness, and will probably receive the artillery tonight, although the Engineers, I believe, did not speculate on their being ready to open fire till the 21st.

The 1st Division of artillery reached the park last night from Elvas, and the remainder will come up before the batteries can be ready for them. The whole consists of 62 pieces—*viz.* sixteen 24-prs; thirty 18-prs., and sixteen 5½-inch heavy iron howitzers. The calculation, I understand, is that we shall have the place in one-and-twenty days, reckoning from the 17th. Fort St. Christoval is not thought of, and on that side we have only a corps of Portuguese upon the Caia, to cover and protect our bridges, which are established a little below its junction with the Guadiana.

General Graham, with the 1st, 6th, and 7th Divisions, would be at Tapa yesterday, from which he would drive Drouet, should he not have abandoned it. The 1st Division of cavalry is also with this corps. Hill is at Merida, and the 5th Division, which was left to aid in putting Ciudad Rodrigo in a state of security, will join us in a day or two. I am told it would reach Portalegre on the 16th or 17th. As yet we have had very bad weather, but I hope its fury is nearly spent; if so, we shall rather have benefitted than otherwise by the dark and stormy nights in commencing works. I have heard nothing certain with regard to the efforts of the enemy to collect; but should Lord Wellington's calculations be as just as they were respecting the enemy's means of relieving Rodrigo, we may expect a happy result to our present operations.

I am told that he is very sanguine, and that Fletcher is so likewise. I will continue to apprise you of the events that may occur here. At present I have it only in my power to thank you for your letter of the 18th. February, to beg your excuse for this hasty scrawl, and to offer my affectionate regards to your family and my friends around you.

P.S.—The enemy are said to have a garrison of 4500 men, and the place has been very much strengthened since our last efforts against it. Lord Wellington comes into camp to fix headquarters today.

To Sir Hew Dalrymple.

Camp before Badajos,
March 27, 1812.

My dear Sir,

I had scarcely closed my letter of the 19th, when our attention was engaged by a sortie made by the enemy against our trenches. It was led by General Vallande (the second in command), and consisted of 1500 infantry and about thirty dragoons. The former succeeded in throwing themselves into our first parallel, but were immediately driven from it with considerable loss, leaving some dead and wounded behind them; they, however, contrived to carry off about 200 intrenching tools, but did no injury whatever to our work. Our loss, I believe, may be estimated at about ninety killed and wounded, theirs more than double, by the best information we can get.

Whilst this was going on, the dragoons pushed forward, passed through the Engineer Depot, and, separating in small parties, effected their purpose in making a perfect reconnaissance of our camp and preparations. We had not a cavalry man on the ground; they consequently made good their retreat by the right of our trenches, in the same manner as they came out. They took Lieutenant Emmett, of the Engineers, and endeavoured to drag him off, but by his perseverance in resisting, he effected his escape. On this day Lord Wellington moved headquarters from Elvas to camp. On the 20th our infantry had got so well round the fort Picurina, that its artillery was nearly silenced.

On the night of the 23rd the batteries Nos. 1 and 2 were finished, and ten guns taken into them. Four other batteries would have been ready on the night of the 23rd, but owing to the continued bad weather, it was found impracticable. They were completed, and eighteen pieces of artillery taken into them during the night of the 24th. The whole opened fire at ten o'clock on the morning of the 25th, and at nine at night Fort Picurina was carried by assault, the whole garrison being either killed or taken. General Kempt had the conduct of this affair, and it most certainly was one of the most gallant exploits ever performed. The garrison was composed of 237 men, and I believe only about 100 survive. Our loss, I am told, is nearly 300 killed and wounded.

The fort was not breached. It had a ditch of extraordinary depth and wideness, is friezed and palisadoed, and in every respect of uncommon strength; you may, therefore, judge of the gallantry of the troops in overcoming every obstacle, as also an attempted sortie from the Mavelin de St. Roque, made with a view to succour it. I enclose you a hasty tracing of the place, which Jenkinson is running off while I write this, which will enable you to form a better idea of our attack than anything I can say would. Immediately after the fort fell, we broke ground on the second parallel, and before morning had admirable cover.

Yesterday our batteries did little more than ricochet and continue to annoy their defences from No. 3, 4, 5, and 6 batteries, No. 1 and 2 being no longer used, the fort having fallen into our hands. Last night the second parallel was carried on, and the breaching battery commenced on the ground between the Picurina and the bastion Fort Trinidad. It is to consist of fourteen 21-prs. From the night of the 17th till that of the 24th, the rain was almost incessant, by which much inconvenience was suffered, both in the trenches find by the pontoon bridge being so damaged as to be taken up; after which we had only our flying bridge to convey ammunition, provisions, and every supply for the army across the Guadiana for three or four days. A second bridge has since been established, and as the weather promises well, I hope we shall also have the fords open.

It is understood that General Graham and General Hill are endeavouring to cut off Drouet. By the reports we can pick up, they were to move the day before yesterday—the former upon La Serena from Almendralijo, the other from Merida. Our cavalry were at Tape on the 23rd. Drouet is said to have only about 6000 men with him, and I believe he is somewhere between Modellin and the Sierra Morena behind Homachon.

I now, my dear Sir, request you will accept my best thanks for your welcome letter of the 4th March, and may I beg you will offer them for me to Lady Dalrymple, Mrs. Leighton, and my cousins. I am sure they will forgive me for not writing to them, on account of the constant employment I find arising from curiosity and anxiety to see what is going on. I have little or no personal concern in the operation, my troop only furnishing a daily picquet of two guns in rear of the trenches, as a support in case of a sortie.

You will, no doubt, be a little surprised at the strange trap for the reputations of our senior officers the service of this country has been. It was but very lately that General Howorth felt himself under the necessity to withdraw, and upon sitting down before this place, owing to some difference of opinion (we suppose) between Lord Wellington and General Borthwick, he also has left the army for England, and is succeeded by Lieut.-Colonel Framingham, the very officer Lord Wellington applied to have superseded, when in command, previous to Borthwick's coming out. This will surely work some change in our regiment. Report says that Lord Wellington told Borthwick that he wanted an active officer to fill so important a situation as Chief of Artillery, and recommended him to go home.

This may be exaggerated, but we really believe there is some truth in it. We have to regret in his departure the loss of an officer who was held in much esteem by his corps, and lament that his character was not better known to our chief, from whom, I fear, he has not had a fair trial.

Fletcher received a slight wound in the shoulder on the 19th, but did not leave camp, and is doing very well; but I am sorry to say his corps has had another severe loss. Captain Mulcaster, one of the finest fellows I ever knew, fell on the morning of the 25th. Major Macleod has been wounded, but doing well—his leg broken by a musket ball.

To Sir Hew Dalrymple.

Camp Badajos,
April 8, 1812.

My dear Sir,

As the public despatch will convey to you all the details of our operations as soon or sooner than this can reach you, I shall not enter upon them further than to say that, instead of ten guns, as I stated in my letter of the 27th *ult.*, being employed in effecting the breaches, there were at last upwards of thirty; and that, notwithstanding the great distance at which the batteries were established, three breaches were quite practicable—one in the right face of the bastion of La Trinidad, another in the curtain between it and St. Maria, and the third in the left flank of the last-named bastion; but, unfortunately, owing to our irregular mode of attack in not carrying it on to the crest of the glacis, and establishing ourselves on the covered way, the enemy availed himself of our distance from him to form such defences for the breaches, that, from what I can learn, they were decidedly the strongest part of this fortress.

This I hope will be related in the despatch, in justice to the troops employed against them and to our corps, as well as the Engineers, who, labouring under the usual want of means, it is said were unwilling to undertake the operation of sapping and mining, which would have been necessary without proper artificers, which they have not.

I was unlucky enough to get a blow on the forehead with a grape shot, which, although I suffer no inconvenience from it, has induced me to lay up for a few days at the instance of the surgeons, that I may not be plagued by any future annoyance from it. It luckily struck the leather peak of my cap, which turned the ball, but laid the bone bare without doing it any injury. One unfortunate fellow close beside me, whose skull was not quite so impenetrable, received the ball, and fell by it. The scratch on mine is already looking so well, that in a few days I shall be well as ever.

Indeed I should not have thought of mentioning it, but that I know that one's family are often made uneasy by the idle communications of friends, although not named in the list of real sufferers; and never was there a more melancholy one than that which will be presented to the weeping eyes of the mourners for the noble fellows who have met a glorious death in this sad though gallant affair. Poor General M'Leod has lost his eldest son, than whom there was not a better officer in the service. His second son, whose leg was broken in the beginning of the siege, is, I am happy to say, doing well. Soult, we hear, has fallen back a little since the place fell, but Marmont is still reported to be in earnest in his threat against Rodrigo.

General Bradford called upon me yesterday, and, I am glad to say, looking very well. He seems pleased with his brigade.

As I am in some measure transgressing orders in not keeping my pate constantly wet, by which application I am promised my full liberty in a few days, I shall beg of you to shew this to my aunt.

The private journal, from which extracts have been given for the years 1809 and 1810, becomes again available from the 11th April, 1812, three days after the date of the last letter:—

April 11th, 1812.—An order is received at 2 in the morning for the Light and 3rd Divisions to march at 7 o'clock to Campo Mayor.

April 26th, Sunday.—The division goes into quarters. . . . Downman comes up.

May 9th.—Macdonald joins from England.

May 11th.—Ride with Macdonald and Blatchley to Ciudad Rodrigo.

May 12th.—Mr. Collins reports his having joined to take charge as commissary to my troop.

May 15th.—My troop inspected by Major-General Count Alten, who has been appointed to the command of the division. Dine at headquarters.

May 25th.—Accompany Blatchley to look at Puerta de Parales. The route quite passable for any carriages.

May 27th.—Lord Wellington reviews the Light Division, including my troop, on ground near Guinalvo, at half-past 5 in the morning.

The entries which follow relate to the movements of the army before the Battle of Salamanca, and at its entry into Madrid:—

1812. June 16th.—The three columns continued their march on their different routes to the heights of Salamanca, skirmished with and drove in the enemy's columns to the banks of the River Tormes.

June 17th.—The enemy were ascertained to have retired in the night, and the 3rd Division crossed the ford of Los Cantos on the Tormes—the 1st, 6th, and 7th, and Light Divisions, and cavalry, at that of St. Martha. The enemy patrolled back towards Salamanca with 87 squadrons of cavalry. A garrison was left by them in their fort, consisting of 700 or 800 men.

June 18th.—The Light Division advanced on the Toro road to Monté Torbias, a league from Salamanca. The batteries against the fort are commenced.

June 19th.—The batteries against the fort opened.

June 20th.—Marmont advanced with 15,000 men, and our army took up a position to cover Salamanca, about one league from it, with their right on the Tormes, and left secured by Marmont being unable to extend too much to his right, and thereby uncover the Madrid and Toro roads.

June 21st and 22nd.—Marmont reconnoitred our position very closely, but withdrew from before it on the night of the 22nd.

June 23rd.—In the evening, Marmont was discovered making a flank movement towards our right, extending his left to Huerta, on the Tormes. The Light Division moved to the right of the position. An attempt made by the 6th Division to storm the forts, but failed.

June 24th.—Bock's cavalry passed the river. The enemy crossed the Tormes above Huerta, with about 10,000 men; but Sir Thomas Graham having crossed at St. Martha with the 1st and 7th Divisions, the enemy recrossed to Huerta at night.

June 25th.—Both armies remained quiet.

June 26th.—Ditto. Our batteries opened again against the fort, and set fire to the convent with red-hot shot.

June 27th.—The two small forts carried by assault, and the main one surrendered at discretion. Marmont retired towards Valladolid in the night.

June 28th.—Nothing extraordinary. The Light Division moved from the position to Moresco and Castellanos.

June 29th.—The army moved forward in three columns. General Alten's cavalry, the Light. 1st, 5th, and 7th Divisions, with Pack's Brigade, composed the centre column, and marched on Ravada de Tubiales. The heavy Germans (Bock's) and 4th Division formed the right column and moved on the road. Anson's Brigade, the 3rd and 6th Division, Bradford's Portuguese, Don Carlos and Don Julian with their corps, composed the left column and marched upon the road to P——.

June 30th.—The columns, with some alterations in their strength, continued their routes on the Valladolid, Tondrecillas, and Toro roads. The Light Division at ——

July 1st.—The Light Division, Anson's Cavalry, at Nave del Rey.

July 2nd.—The Light Division and cavalry halted at Rueda—headquarters.

July 3rd.—The Light Division and two brigades of cavalry threatened the bridge of Tordesillas over the Douro, whilst the 3rd Division and Don Julian's cavalry forced the ford of Polios with little loss.

July 14th.—March at dusk to camp at Foncastin.

July 15th.—March at dusk to Castrajon, by Villa Verde, which we reach at daybreak on the 16th.

July 16th.—The enemy make an attack on Castrajon at daybreak, in which affair Belson is wounded, two horses killed and one wounded, and Gunner Rotton is slightly wounded. We hold our ground till the arrival of Lord Wellington, who orders us to fall back upon the position of Canazal. The 4th Division is attacked in the evening, but repulses the enemy. The hussars and 14th Dragoons also make a very gallant charge.

July 18th.—Remain in position.

July 19th.—The enemy make a movement at 3 p.m. to our right, which compels us to cross the Guazeña at Vallesa, thereby causing them to make a considerable detour to gain our right. They shew a disposition to force the passages of a ford, which induces Sir S. Cotton to order my troop into action, when Lieut. Smith is severely wounded, one horse killed, and two others wounded.

July 20th.—The enemy still continues to manoeuvre upon our right flank. Both armies march at daybreak, and move the whole day within sight of each other, and occasionally exchanging a cannonade. They march on Villaruela and Huerta, whilst we move by Cantalpino, Espedron, Pittugua, and Aldea Lingua. We push a corps on to the latter place to secure the fords below it, whilst the enemy make a similar exertion to gain Huerta.

July 21st.—We march before daybreak, and occupy nearly the position we did when covering the siege of Salamanca, extending from St. Christoval to Aldea Lingua. The enemy are nearly in their former position. In the afternoon they are discovered to be in motion towards Alba de Tormes, and to be crossing the fords between that place and Huerta. We also march, and the whole army, excepting the 3rd Division, which remains in front of Salamanca, cross to St. Martha, extending itself along the heights towards Calvalrasa.

July 22nd.—The enemy, continuing to manoeuvre upon our right flank, march soon after daybreak, and it being ascertained that the whole of their force had crossed the Tormes, Lord Wellington places his army in position, brings over the 3rd Division, which he holds in reserve, and awaits the effect of their movements, when, seeing a favourable opportunity, he attacks them. The brunt of the battle falls upon the 3rd Division (which turns the enemy's left), the 5th, 6th, and 4th British Divisions, and General Le Marchant's cavalry.

They are completely routed, losing nearly 6000 prisoners, about 2000 killed, besides the wounded carried off. The 1st and Light Division and 7th Division were not engaged. The two first are ordered to pursue, and the enemy are driven without an attempt at a stand. Favoured, however, by the woody country, they gain the bridge of Alba de Tormes; whilst Lord Wellington, depending upon its being secured by the Spaniards, directs our march upon Huerta. The action finished with daylight, and we continued the pursuit until past twelve at night. Headquarters and advance guard at Calvalrasa.

July 23rd.—March at daybreak, General Bock's cavalry and the Light Division forming the advance guard. The former come up with the enemy at La Serna, and are immediately directed to charge, which they perform admirably, taking about 1500 prisoners, one piece of artillery, and an ammunition waggon. Halt at Hocvillas.

July 24th.—March with the cavalry to Cabeca de Pazor. Come up with the enemy, who retire *en masse,* covering their rear with 22 squadrons of cavalry. Our force too small, and without infantry, they go off unmolested.

July 25th.—The whole army halt

Aug. 12th.—Lord Wellington enters Madrid. Downman and myself meant to have witnessed his entrance, and for that purpose left the castle of the Escurial in the morning—the Light and 1st Divisions having halted there—but met his lordship returning to fix his head-quarters at Las Rozas. Learn that Macdonald had three guns taken and destroyed on the 11th by the enemy's cavalry. This loss is justly attrib-uted to the misconduct of the Portuguese cavalry, and took place near the village of Las Rozas. The enemy retired from Madrid on that day, leaving a garrison in the Retiro and La China. The joy and acclama-tions of the inhabitants of Madrid on their release from French power is not to be described, and their attention and hospitality to the British army cannot be excelled.

Aug. 13th.—Lord Wellington fixes headquarters in the Palacio de Rey. Reconnoitres the Retiro and La China.

Light Division marches to Las Rozas and ——. I accompany Downman to Madrid with Macdonald, where we find Gardiner. Visit the palace and the Palacio el Principe del Pace.

Colonel Burgoyne is sent to communicate with the governor, who refuses to surrender, and, in consequence, the outer wall which sur-rounds the La China Port at a distance and connects with the Retiro, is broken in at several places after dark.

The pipes conveying the principal supply of water to the fort cut off; and as the troops occupying the Retiro are in danger of being cut off from any relief, the governor withdraws them within the works of La China, leaving a large supply of powder, stores, clothing, &c, which is taken possession of at daylight.

Aug. 14th.—The 7th. and 3rd Divisions ordered for the assault in the morning; but the governor offering to surrender, a capitulation is drawn up. The whole to be prisoners of war; to lay down their arms on the glacis; the officers retaining their horses and baggage, the men their knapsacks. Two thousand and upwards effective men are marched off at four o'clock in the evening, and there are 300 or 400 sick, unfit to move, 203 pieces of artillery (principally French), nearly 20,000 stand of arms (nine of them English), and clothing for 10,000 men, besides an immense quantity of ammunition, timber, iron, and every sort of stores, and two eagles are found in the place. Light Division moves to Villa Verda. Go to the opera.

Aug. 15th.—The new Constitution of Spain is proclaimed, and received by the people with marks of the greatest enthusiasm. A public ball is given to Lord Wellington in consequence of the happy event. Visit the museum, the opera, and ball.

Aug. 16th.—Join my troop at Villa Verda.

Aug. 19th.—Troop moves into quarters at the Retiro, Madrid.

Sept. 1st.—Headquarters move to the Escurial, on the way to the Douro. General Alten left with the Light and 3rd Divisions, and Don Carlos D'Espana at Madrid, and the 4th at the Escurial.

Sept. 7th.—Smith joins from Salamanca.

Sept. 24th.—Blachley marches for Burgos, to join his troop.

Nov. 11th.—Parker arrives here with the reserve 9-pr. Brigade.

Nov. 14th.—The enemy march upon Alba de Tormes and the upper fords, in consequence of which we cross the bridge of Salamanca, and march to the position of Arepilos.

Nov. 15th.—The enemy having crossed their whole army, and marching by our right towards Tamames, we retire across the Valmosa, where we bivouac.

Nov. 16th.—Continue our retreat across the Huebra.

Nov. 17th.—At San Muños, where the enemy come up with the rear guard (Light Division). A sharp skirmish takes place, in which Captain Dawson, 52nd, is killed, and Rideout, 43rd, mortally wounded, Major McDonald severely wounded, and on this day General Sir

G. Paget is taken prisoner. I lose my pie horse by a gun shot, and three men wounded.

Nov. 18th.—Cross the Yeltes at Santie Spiritus.

Nov. 19th.—Arrive at Ciudad Rodrigo. Assistant Commissary Lawrie joins.

Dec 7th.—Accompany Cator to hunt, who kills his horse by the chase.

Dec 8th.—Colonel Fisher arrives at headquarters to command artillery.

Dec 12th.—Lord Wellington leaves Freneda for Cadiz.

The following are extracts from Major Ross's letters of this year to Sir Hew Dalrymple:—

Camp, Monté Tubias, in front of Salamanca,
June 18, 1812.

My dear Sir,

As I stated in my letter of the 9th, the army was put in motion on the 11th. The advance guard (composed of the Light Division and 1st Hussars), under General Charles Alten, crossing the Agueda, and the rest halting to assemble on the left bank. On the 12th, the whole remained on their ground, and the regiments and detachments lately landed from England joined their respective corps and divisions on the 13th. We commenced our march upon Salamanca in three columns—the centre being formed of the advance guard, the 4th and 5th Divisions, and two brigades of heavy cavalry and one of light. The headquarters moved with it. The left column was under General Picton, and consisted of the 3rd Division, Pack's and Bradford's Portuguese Brigades, and the 11th Dragoons. That of the right was under General Graham, who had the 1st, 6th, and 7th Divisions, and the 14th Light Dragoons.

On the 16th, the heads of the columns arrived to a minute on the little river, the Valmuza, where we found the enemy's picquets, which were immediately driven in, and in a few hours their cavalry, which had occupied the heights, were compelled to fall back upon their infantry under the walls of Salamanca, and at night they crossed the bridge, and marched on the road towards Toro, leaving garrisons in the three forts they have constructed on a part of the town which they destroyed for the purpose, levelling all the houses within 300 yards of their ports, with the exception of a convent enclosed in one of them, which they have made strong by means of loopholes, &c. Yesterday morning we marched before daybreak to invest the place by the fords above and below the town, which was immediately occupied by the 6th Division, and this morning we moved up to this place from the Tormes, where all the infantry were last night. Already Colonel Burgoyne has commenced operations against the forts, and I was told that batteries would be ready today for four 18-pounders which have accompanied the army from Rodrigo, and six iron howitzers which Colonel Dickson is bringing by the pass of Parales from the Alentejo, and which it is expected will reach Salamanca today.

From my own observation and what I have heard, I should think we shall very soon be masters of these works; but whether it is the intention of Lord Wellington to wait till they fall, or move the army forward, I cannot guess; but this much appears very certain—that the sooner we can force Marmont to fight the better, for there can be no question that time is strength to him. It seems to be the prevailing opinion, that he will make his stand on the Douro; but opposed to this, one must take into consideration that the Gallician Army are said to be advancing, and the militia under Trant and Leloricio, with some Portuguese cavalry, are moving from Tras os Montés upon Formoza. The companies of artillery I mentioned in my last have sailed some time ago from the Tagus for Gibraltar, from whence I trust ere this they have gone on to their destination.

It has just occurred to me that I never answered a question you put in a former letter regarding the melancholy and numerous casualties in the Engineers. It is by no means my opinion that it has arisen from the nature of their uniforms but from that high sense of honour and gallantry that has so particularly shone in the lamented individuals of that distinguished corps. With the exception of poor Mulcaster, all have fallen when on night duty; consequently, it must be attributed to their forward situation, not to their coat. You will have seen with regret the account of poor Squire's death. He is a very great loss to his country, for he possessed very great zeal and superior talents, and it is melancholy that he should just have attained his highest ambition by the recent promotions when called to that state where such honours are of no avail.

You will, I am sure, excuse my here taking leave for the present, and also any confusion there may appear in the above recital, for I am ready to fall asleep from an early march, and, besides, I have not more than time to send this off for the packet. Headquarters are in Salamanca.

Aldea Mayor near Tudelo de Douro,
August 3, 1812.

My dear Sir,

Although I cannot hope to offer you any intelligence respecting our late operations that you will not have received in a more detailed and accurate form from the official accounts, yet I cannot let the only recent opportunity of a regular communication pass without writing, and may I request you will have the goodness to forward the enclosed to my sister when you find it convenient. In a hasty letter I sent Fanshawe on the 24th (the contents of which I begged he would make known to you), I noticed the fortunate result of the two days previous; but whether or not that letter may reach him appears doubtful, as I sent it at a hazard, though pretty sure it would not be allowed to precede the official carrier, who I have since learnt did not leave the army for some days after. It is much to be regretted that, owing to the continued and close manoeuvring of the two armies for several days previous to the action, it was rendered necessary to keep our commissariat supplies considerably in our rear, owing to which our future advance was unavoidably retarded; for had it been otherwise, I am fully satisfied we might, with a very inferior force, have totally destroyed Marmont's broken and dispirited army.

Lord Wellington, however, seemed resolved neither to harass his army or run any risk of its being without supplies, and the consequence has been that they have scrambled off—though certainly, from every account, in a most lamentable state, with hardly a sound General left to conduct them. Numerous have been the reports that Marmont had died of his wounds, but I think without foundation; as, from the last information we could get at Tudela, from whence we (the Light Division) marched last night, though dangerously ill, he still nominally commanded the army, which has marched by different roads upon Burgos. On the night of the 29th they destroyed the stores they could not convey from Valladolid, and leaving 800 sick, abandoned the city. Colonel Ponsonby, with the 12th Dragoons, immediately entered, as did the Guerilla Martini; and soon after daybreak the greater part of our army moved Upon the ford of Hezzera, but only the Light Division and some cavalry crossed the Douro.

Lord Wellington visited the place, but re-crossed the river in the evening, and the next day moved his headquarters to Cuellar, having previously marched some divisions in that direction for the purpose of beating Joseph, or at all events preventing his junction with Marmont. I have heard this morning that he had yesterday some expectation of being able to fall upon him at Leguara in the morning, but His Majesty had prudently taken himself off for Madrid in the night, carrying an immense booty, which he levied upon the inhabitants in the shape of a contribution. At this moment our army is so strangely disposed, that I cannot place any part of it except this division, which marched last night late from Tudelo, crossing the Douro to this place. Headquarters are at Cuellar, and I am told two or three divisions are near it, and the 1st Division between that place and this.

The cavalry are everywhere. It is fruitless speculating upon our future movements, so various are the views in which they may be taken; but was I to guess at anything, I should say Lord Wellington will content himself for the present with what has been done; for the weather is grown horridly hot, and the troops are suffering a little in health, which would be a serious evil if it increased, and we moved much further from our hospitals, looking forward, as I still think we must, to the impossibility of our holding a more advanced position than we now do. What an incalculable misfortune at this juncture is the failure of Lord William Bentink's co-operation in the south. Had it taken place, our prospects would have been commanding indeed; as it is, I very much fear our force is not adequate to the destruction of the armies that can be brought against us, and probably the most we can hope for is the raising the siege of Cadiz.

I have a letter this morning from James Ross, from Tapa, where General Hill still had his headquarters. We have a great interest in hearing what effect Marmont's defeat will have upon the southern armies. . . . We have heard of three car loads of English letters leaving Ciudad Bodrigo for the army, but as they are drawn by bullocks, whilst following the restless life we have done of late, there is little prospect of our benefitting by the correspondence of our friends. The cause of this tardy proceeding is the difficulty of transport, for the French have hardly left an animal in the country they have retired through.

Madrid,
August 30, 1812.

My dear Sir,

The inhabitants of this city have throughout shewn themselves truly patriotic and warm in the cause we are engaged in; but, notwith-standing the best efforts are making to form and organise an armed force, I think there is but very little chance of its ever being an efficient one in the face of an enemy, because it will be quite impossible to pro-cure fit subjects for officers—so wretchedly deficient is this country of the class qualified to hold the situations. Most of the *noblesse* and respectable gentlemen are absent, either in France with Joseph or at Cadiz; and whatever their inclinations may be, I fear it will be a long time ere they consider our footing sufficiently secure to induce them to return. Don Carlos is acting as governor of the provinces lately gained, in the absence of Castanos, and I believe is conducting mat-ters as well as can be expected; and if the people can be brought to add energy to good will, I think we have the best prospect open to us.

In the movement Lord Wellington is now making towards the Douro, I conjecture he only aims at getting rid of Marmont's forces by sending them back previous to some decided co-operation with Hill and Maitland; as, whilst our divisions have been crossing the Gua-darrama, preparation is making here to throw a bridge across the Tagus at Almaraz; and it is, I believe, quite certain that the 3rd Division, and probably the Light, will remain in Madrid during the movements making by the rest of the army. The situation of the army at present is: the 6th and 5th in the neighbourhood of Arevalo; the 1st have their route, commencing this day, for the same place; and the 4th and 7th are still at the Escurial, from whence the 1st are to march. All the cav-alry, except the 1st Hussars and 14th (which are on the Toledo road), are long since on the other side of the Guadarrama

We have been much indebted to King Joseph for many comforts in letting us have Madrid uninjured, and the service has been much benefitted by his arsenals, which we got full of every sort of store, and from which we have been very busy in making a complete refit of all our brigades of artillery, the carriages of which we have nearly renewed.

Madrid,
October 18, 1812.

My dear Sir,

The last English mail which reached us only a few days back brought me your letter of the 10th September, which I seize the first opportunity of answering, that I may apologise for my long silence, and, as far as I can, account for it, which I can do no otherwise than by acknowledging that I have found the novelty of being in the enjoyment of good quarters and every other luxury much too powerful an inducement to idleness. This is an excuse (a bad one I own) which I expect very soon to be deprived of; at least there appears every prospect of our immediate march towards the Tagus. Chinchilla has surrendered, and I understand that Soult has again made an advance to Albacete.

Two carriers passed through yesterday from Sir R. Hill to Lord Wellington, and it is said they communicate Sir Rowland's opinion that the enemy has at length fixed upon his plan of operation, and that his movements indicate an intention of marching towards us. Should this intelligence prove true, we expect that the marquis will join us immediately, leaving Sir G. Paget in command of the corps in the north.

Our force here will be very respectable, particularly when General Skerret with the troops from Cadiz shall have joined. They are today at Talavera la Rena, and as far as I can learn, the whole will assemble on the Jerama, which is a good position; General Hill's corps falling back from the Tagus, whilst the Light, 3rd, and 4th Divisions move up from this city and its neighbourhood, our present cantonments.

The force of the enemy is so variously stated, that I am afraid to guess at it; but I think it is generally believed that, if really in earnest in his seeming threat to try his strength with us, he cannot bring more than 45,000 or 50,000, as he must necessarily leave a corps to observe Alicante, and must at the same time have an eye towards the numerous Spanish corps that hang about him, but from whose exertions I fear he has very little to apprehend; and it is reported here this morning that one of them has been completely dispersed already. True or not, I cannot tell, but the Spaniards, who have generally good information, say that General Dalmaguer has routed Bassecourt's force.

The unfortunate failure of all our efforts against Burgos, has been a sad blow to the flattering prospects we indulged our hopes in. Nothing, I should think, could prove more injurious to us than the delay it has occasioned; and I don't hear that we are yet by any means certain of getting it into our possession, though Lord Wellington seems resolved to overcome every difficulty, and to have it at all hazards and at any cost.

Why he should have undertaken the siege of such a place with means so very inadequate appears very extraordinary, especially as there was little or no difficulty in augmenting it to any extent, either from the guns and ammunition found here, or from the ships from St.

Andero.

At the commencement of the siege, he had only three 18-prs. and eight 24-pr. iron howitzers, and not more than three days' expenditure of ammunition. My last letter from thence, dated the 13th, gives no very pleasing account of the state of the battering train at that time, and I have not heard that it has been since improved. Two of the three 18-prs. have lost their trunnions, and the other struck twelve times by the enemy's shot.

The two former, by dint of invention and experiment, Colonel Dickson has contrived to mount on carriages constructed on purpose; and all the 24-pr. shot being expended, we have been firing 18-pr. shot from the 24-pr. howitzers with tolerable effect. For the last three days we have fired hot shot at the convent; but although we have battered in the roof, it will not take fire; I therefore fear the materials are not of a burning nature.

Perhaps while I am writing the place may be ours, but I confess I am not very sanguine; and even should you have later accounts from thence than this will convey, I am sure you will excuse me for giving you the foregoing extract, which will at least show you the poverty of means our corps have had to work with; and even if his lordship should deal with us after his usual cold manner in his report of the affair, I trust that you will believe that those who have been employed in it have not been wanting in zeal and exertion.

The Engineers have again had their full share of loss; Captain Williams killed, and Lieut.-Colonel Jones, an excellent officer, shot through the ankle. The artillery have also had some casualties, though none killed; Captains Dansey and Power and Lieutenant Elgee have each been wounded.

Poor Cox, of the 79th, is a most severe loss to the army. He certainly was an officer of the highest promise, and I really believe the best dragoon in the service. In short, this vile place, Burgos, has been a source of extreme mortification, and has caused more anxiety than I have known to be felt at any former period. Perhaps this is to be accounted for by the check it has given us in the midst of our highest exultation.

The following extract contains a vindication of the Light Division in general, and of the Chestnut Troop in particular, from a censure passed by Lord Wellington on the conduct of the troops after the Battle of Salamanca:—

To his sister

Aldea del Obespo,
February 16, 1813.

I perceive by your letter, as well as the observations in the news-papers, that you all think your army in this country forgot themselves very much in the retreat from Salamanca. Be assured it is thought much worse of than it deserves; and although Lord Wellington's cir-cular is a general censure upon all, it does not with justice affect more than two or three divisions. The 'Light' is perfectly clear of meriting it in any way, and his lordship's remark at his own table is a proof of this. The letter became the subject of conversation, when Colonel Barnard, who commands one of the brigades, said, 'We do not take it to ourselves,' and was immediately replied to, 'I know that; I never intended you should.' With regard to my own troop, I had not a fault to find, nor could anyone else do so during the whole time. You must not, therefore, suppose that the letter, which appears so harsh in the papers, has had the effect of annoying any but those who ought to feel it, though I must say it would have been less prejudicial to the char-acter of the army and more equitable to individuals had the censure been applied only to those generals and commanding officers of regi-ments whose want of ability or exertion allowed those under them to relax in their discipline.

The next letter is one to Major Ross, from his 2nd Captain, Cap-tain Jenkinson, enclosing a copy of the prince regent's answer to a memorial of the 2nd Captains of the Royal Artillery on the subject of their exclusion from brevet promotion.

The subject is of such interest to artillery officers, that the letter and memorial and the correspondence attached to it are given in full.

Dear Ross,

I wrote to you not an hour ago, since which the answer to the me-morial of the 2nd Captains has arrived. A copy of it is written within, and you will perceive fully grants the prayer of our petition.

I have not time for more, for I am going to send Ramsay, Whiny-ates, Cairnes, and Dyneley a copy, and I shall desire Whinyates to show it to Webber.

Believe me
Your sincere and affectionate friend,
George Jenkinson.

Fisher is, of course, delighted; and, indeed, he and the peer merit our warmest thanks. He means to thank the peer in our name the next time he sees him.

The memorial of the 2nd Captains of the Royal Artillery serving under the Marquess of Wellington, 1813:—

This memorial humbly sheweth that the 2nd Captains of the Royal Artillery serving in the Peninsula have not, on account of their regimental commission, obtained that brevet promotion given to other captains in His Majesty's army, when their services have been thought by the Commander of the Forces to merit public notice in his despatches.

"They humbly hope, therefore, that when their case is fairly laid before your Royal Highness, you may be graciously pleased to grant to them that advantage of brevet promotion which it must be ever the utmost pride of a soldier to obtain for his services.

The commission which your Royal Highness's memorialists bear runs thus:—'That from the date of this, our commission, you shall take rank as a captain in the army and 2nd Captain in the Royal Regiment of Artillery;' upon which regimental rank is founded the objection to giving them brevet rank, when mentioned as having distinguished themselves, whilst younger captains of other regiments obtain promotion for similar mention in the same despatch, as in the cases of Ciudad Rodrigo and Badajos, and all the subsequent events of the late memorable campaign.

Your Royal Highness's memorialists have only humbly to request that, before the commencement of the ensuing campaign, your Royal Highness may be graciously pleased to take their case into your consideration; and that should your Royal Highness consider those 2nd Captains of the Royal Artillery mentioned as having distinguished themselves in the late campaign to have equally merited promotion with younger captains in the army who have received it, that your Royal Highness may be pleased to direct that, on any future occasion, should the services of any of your memorialists be thought entitled to the public notice of the Commander of the Forces, that the door to promotion may be open to them, and that their regimental rank may no longer exclude them from that which is the pride and hope of the least ambitious soldier.

Signed by

E. C. Whinyates,	W. Cator,
W. N. Ramsay,	C. Dansey,
G. Jenkinson,	A. Thompson,

W. Power,	B. Wills,
W. Green,	E. Michell,
R. M. Cairnes,	W. Webber,
T. Dyneley,	A. M. Macdonald."
J. Parker,	

Colonel Fisher to Marquess of Wellington.

My Lord,

In presuming to request your lordship to lay the enclosed memorial before His Royal Highness the Prince Regent of England, the 2nd Captains serving under your lordship's command in this country would not presume to take that liberty, were it not for your lordship's well-known attention to any cases of hardship which may be considered as existing in the army under your command.

The memorial which they have the honour to enclose is not founded on your lordship's supposed approbation of the services of any of those who have signed it, but upon the mention of some of them in your lordship's public despatches after the captures of Ciudad Rodrigo and Badajos, and some subsequent events of the late brilliant campaign.

The 2nd Captains in the Royal Artillery who were thought by your lordship to have distinguished themselves in those operations, were classed with 1st Captains of their own regiments, and younger captains of others, who received that brevet promotion which, on account of their regimental rank, was denied to them. Trusting, therefore, that your lordship will see how grating it must be to the feelings of any soldiers to find themselves without a hope of reward, whatever may be the nature of their services, and however much they may be considered to merit the approbation of the officers they are serving under, they anxiously hope that your lordship will lend the powerful aid of your recommendation to their case; that should any of them be fortunate enough in the ensuing campaign to be publicly mentioned by your lordship, it may obtain for them that brevet promotion which has hitherto been alone withheld from them.

Sir Henry Torrens to Lord Wellington.

Horse Guards,
March 3, 1813.

My Lord,

I have not failed to submit to the commander-in-chief your lordship's despatch of the 28th January, covering the letter addressed to your lordship and the memorial addressed to the prince regent from the 2nd Captains of artillery serving in the army under your lordship's command.

I have the commands of His Royal Highness to assure your lordship that the distinctions under which he had thought himself called upon to exclude 2nd Captains of Engineers and Artillery from his recommendations to the regent for brevet promotion, did not originate in any want of a due impression of the merits of several individuals who have distinguished themselves in that rank under your lordship's command. But although it was necessary at the time to draw a line of distinction in such cases, yet His Royal Highness is sorry to find that it has borne hard upon certain individuals who might otherwise have had the advantage of your lordship's notice.

Upon a consideration of the *whole case,* however, His Royal Highness will submit the memorial for the gracious and favourable consideration of the prince regent, in order that your lordship *may in future be enabled* to recommend for *brevet rank* such *Second* Captains of Engineers and Artillery whose conduct shall merit your notice and protection.

(Signed)   H. Torrens.

The time was now approaching for another and more active campaign than any our troops had taken part in in the Peninsula.

On the 10th May, Major Ross writes to his sister:—

Puebla de Azava,
May 10, 1813.

N. Ramsay is quite well, and marching the troop which he commands by Oporto, through the north of Portugal, towards Spain. We all expect to march in about a week or ten days. The army are in the highest health and good order, and much stronger than at the opening of any former campaign; and as the enemy are much weaker in number (and we may suppose in spirit also), it is not, I think, too much to assume when I say that we shall carry it all our own way, and that you will not hear of much, if any, fighting; indeed, the common opinion is that they will retire from us. Should matters turn out as I certainly hope they will, I hope to take shipping a few months hence from some of the northern ports of Spain for England, instead of by the old route of Lisbon.

May 18th.—. . . . I shall only add that I am quite well, and tell you that we were reviewed yesterday by Lord Wellington, when my troop came in for its share of praise. We expect to march in a few days.

The Light Division, to which Major Ross's troop remained attached, marched on the 21st May.

The journal of the 18th June records its first encounter with the enemy:—

June 18th.—By La Bovida to San Millan, where the Light Division fall upon General Maucune's division, takes all his baggage and 300 prisoners; after which, move on to Villa Nuevo.

June 19th.—By Espejo and Salines to Pobes. The 4th Division drive the enemy.

June 20th, Sunday.—Halt.

A letter of this day's date to Captain (afterwards General) Fanshawe, of the Royal Engineers, gives a view of the situation of the army the day before the Battle of Vittoria:—

> Camp Near Pobes, four leagues from Vittoria,
> June 20, 1813.

My dear Fanshawe,

Since I wrote to you on the 13th, we have been marching every day, and almost the whole day, through such a country as few armies have attempted to go over, and I really believe none ever performed the like and suffered less. We are now in possession of all the passes looking into the plains of Vittoria, and this evening the whole army will be close up, ready to pour into it, which we (the ignorant) expect will take place tomorrow morning.

On the 18th, the Light Division came suddenly from Loga, by the Pass of Bovida, upon the division of Maucune, whilst in column of march through San Millan from Frias towards Espejo, and completely overset it. The whole of the baggage fell into our hands with about 400 prisoners, and the remainder of a brigade broke and fled singly into the mountains, where they are supposed now to be wandering; and Morilla, with his Spanish corps, has been sent to pick up what he can.

Yesterday, we moved from San Millan to this ground, where we were to have joined in an attack made by the 4th Division (which had marched by a pass on our left) upon two divisions of the enemy posted at La Puebla de Argauzon, and which held a strong pass near this place; but upon a reconnaissance made by Lord Wellington, it was found that a very strong column was marching within a league of us by the great road from Miranda to Vittoria, and as we had not any other divisions near enough to bring to our support, his lordship contented himself with pushing them through the pass with the 4th Division, the mouth of which they took possession of, and the intention of our attacking their flank and rear was given up, after we had moved for the purpose.

As yet, I have not heard a certain opinion as to the intended movements of the enemy. Some think they will stand in the position they got into last night, on this side of Vittoria, whilst others say they will fall back upon France; there is also a probability of their going to Pampeluna, where, I understand, there is a strong position, as well as three fortresses to support them. Of all this, we shall know more in a few days. It cannot be supposed that the march of such an army through so difficult a country, and with such dispatch, could be accomplished without some privations; but they have been trifling, and they have in no way injured the health, order, or equipment of the army, and as the communication is open with St. Andree, we shall be plentifully supplied.

We yesterday heard the French account of the battles in Germany, and the report they have of an armistice, which seems too probable and too provoking to think of. If it is true, their army in this country will soon be reinforced, and our efforts prove fruitless; but I will still hope that it is unfounded, and that a better fate awaits us.

The Battle of Vittoria occurred on the 21st June, the day after this letter was written. The entries of this period, in Major Ross's journal, give few details, but those there are, with the letters which follow, will be read with interest:—

June 21st, Monday.—March at daybreak. The army assembled in front of the enemy, and the attack commenced on the left, by Morillo and General Hill, at a quarter before nine; that of the 4th, Light, and 3rd Divisions, in succession, about eleven o'clock. The enemy were driven from all their positions by three o'clock, and the pursuit only finished with night.

June 22nd.—March in pursuit of the enemy. General von Alten's cavalry and Light Division, forming the advance guard, come up with them at dark, two leagues beyond Salvatierra.

June 23rd.—Continue our march, and cannonade the column of the enemy during the day, as far as Huerte Conguil. The division not being up, my troop remains with the cavalry.

June 24th.—Continue the pursuit, and cannonade the enemy until within a league of Pampeluna. Take an 8-pr., by disabling it with our fire.

★★★★★★

The Duke of Wellington's despatch of the 24th June referred to this pursuit in the following terms:—"We have done them as much injury as has been in our power, considering the state of the roads; and this day the advanced guard, consisting of Major-General Victor Alten's brigade and the 1st and 3rd battalions of the 95th Regiment (now the Rifle Brigade), and Captain Ross's troop of Horse Artillery, took from them the remaining gun they had. They have entered Pampeluna with one howitzer only."

★★★★★★

The letters which follow refer to the battle and pursuit at more length:—

Argandona,
June 22, 1813.

My dear Fanshawe,

I shall try to get this sent by the officer carrying the despatches. I am quite well; tell all my friends so, for I can write to none else, being just going to march. We attacked the enemy yesterday morning at a quarter before nine, and at eight, evening, were in possession of the whole of their artillery. There never was such a rout. Joseph commanded in person, and we have all his baggage, as well as of his whole army, and about a hundred pieces of artillery, some drawn from Burgos and Paucorbo. It is impossible to guess at their killed, wounded, or prisoners, for they are scattered over the whole country.

We are on the march in three columns upon Salvatierra. Hill commands the right, Graham the left, and Lord Wellington the centre. We expect to come up with an immense convoy, which must fall into our hands. They have not a gun left them, and ours are in good order. We have lost a great many men and horses, and have, we flatter ourselves, performed our part in the row.

I can say no more; only give my best affection to all, and pray write to my sisters immediately, to tell them I was never better, and most uncommonly happy by the result of yesterday. All my officers are safe. God bless you, my dear friend, and ever believe me

Your affectionate
(Signed)H. D. R.

72

To Sir Hew Dalrymple.

One and a half leagues from Pampeluna,

June 24, 1813.

My dear Sir,

I lament that I have not had an opportunity of communicating the circumstances attending the glorious action of the 21st; but I have really been so constantly engaged, that it has been quite out of my power. I wrote a few lines to Fanshawe on the morning of the 22nd, which I had hopes would have reached my friends by the same hands that carried home the official despatch, more with a view to tell my friends that I was well than to convey any particulars of the day. The same is the case at present; for I am but just dismounted, after chasing the enemy under the walls of their fortress, and again am desirous of repeating the same piece of information, which I know will be interesting to you and my other friends.

The enemy have continued in full flight ever since their defeat, and I have had the satisfaction of following them close up these two days, keeping a continual cannonade upon their columns, and hurrying them so much as not to give them time to destroy a bridge, though there were many in our march. One (a wooden one), they set on fire; but we got it in time to repair it with ease. 151 pieces of cannon were left on the field on the 21st, with 400 wagons; and today we have taken the only two they had remaining—the last within a league of Pampeluna.

At present, we have only General von Alten's brigade of cavalry, my troop, and the Light Division; and I fancy it will take tomorrow to bring up the rest of the army. This will cause a little delay, otherwise I believe Lord Wellington would continue to press them even to the very place. He certainly does not mean to give them a minute longer than he can help; and I should think there is little doubt of our getting the place, as it cannot possibly be supplied so as to feed an army of 60,000 or 70,000 men, besides its garrison, above a few days; and the army is in such want, that it is to be supposed it will not pass on starving to leave the garrison in a state of defence. That Joseph will risk another battle, I think is quite out of the question without artillery (except what he can get from Pampeluna), and his army dispirited beyond example.

I feel the less concerned in not being able to relate what has come under my own observation, as the despatches will, no doubt, be ample on the occasion of such consequences to ourselves and to Europe.

I had nearly forgotten to mention that General Clausel's corps were in Biscay, and had orders from Joseph to join him on the 22nd at Vittoria. Lord Wellington got intelligence of this, and left Pakenham with the 6th Division there to receive him. He did come, looked at the British corps, but having heard the fate of his friends on the preceding day, he retired, when Pakenham moved from his position to attack him, and is gone on the road to Sarragossa.

P.S.—A report has this instant come in, to be forwarded to Lord Wellington, stating the enemy to be passing Pampeluna, in full march to France.

Major Ross received the brevet rank of Lieut.-Colonel for his services at Vittoria, and was granted a pension of 5s. *per diem* in common with the other commanding officers of divisions and batteries of artillery present in the action, under the following order:—

Tapages de La Velenda,
August 26, 1813.

Artillery Order.

It is with great pleasure that Lieut.-Colonel Dickson (who had succeeded Colonel Fisher in command of the artillery of the army), inserts in orders the following copy of a letter from the Master-General of the Ordnance, in which his lordship communicates the distinguished mark of approbation His Royal Highness the Prince Regent has graciously been pleased to bestow on the artillery officers in command at the Battle of Vittoria, for their services on that occasion.

(Signed)   J. May, A.A.G., R.A.

Extract of a letter from Lord Mulgrave to Lieut.-Colonel Dickson, dated Harley Street, July 16, 1813:—

'On receipt of your letter, addressed to Major-General Macleod, I did not fail to bring under the consideration of the prince regent the very striking and unexampled circumstance of the whole of the British artillery having been brought into action at the Battle of Vittoria, and the whole of the enemy's artillery having been captured in the glorious victory which crowned the exertions of the allies on that ever-memorable occasion. His Royal Highness has been graciously pleased, in consideration of the peculiar circumstances above stated, to mark His Royal Highness's approbation of the particular and successful activity of the corps of Royal Artillery under your orders, by granting severally to the officers intrusted with the command of divisions or brigades an allowance for good service in the following proportions :—To the officers commanding divisions, each 10s. *per diem*; to the officers commanding brigades, each 5s. *per diem*; and to yourself, a similar allowance for good service of 20s. *per diem*.

★★★★★★

A field battery of six guns was then termed a brigade. At an earlier date, guns were attached to battalions of infantry; hence six guns brigaded together grew to be called brigades of field artillery, and two or more brigades under one commanding officer, divisions of artillery. The word "brigade," as used in the field, now signifies the same relative force of artillery as of infantry or cavalry—*viz.* a force of two or more single batteries, though, for administrative purposes, it is applied to larger bodies.

★★★★★★

'In notifying to you His Royal Highness's gracious liberality, I am happy to avail myself of the opportunity of expressing the high sense which I entertain of the distinguished part which the Royal Artillery has borne (on every occasion) in the glorious events which have rendered the war in the Peninsula the brightest epoch in the military history of Great Britain. I beg you to express to the several officers whose names you transmitted to me, my sincere congratulations upon the honourable remuneration which their services have received from the gracious consideration of His Royal Highness the Prince Regent.'

(True copy).

(Signed)   Richard Hardinge,
                          Lieut. and Adjt. R.H.A.

The operations which followed the Battle of Vittoria, from July to the end of the year 1813, were the most active of the war; and in these, Lieut.-Colonel Ross's battery took a most active part.

The letters and journal of this period are inserted according to date, in order to give a clear view of the movements and operations which took place.

To Sir Hew Dairymple.

Narvarte, near San Estevan,
July 10, 1813,

My dear Sirs

In my last of the 24th, I informed you that preparations were making to undertake the siege of Pampeluna. Since then, however, the plan has been changed; and after endeavouring to intercept General Clausel, which his speed prevented, Lord Wellington hurried back

75

from Caseda and Cucastilla to Pampeluna, directed Sir R. D. Hill's corps to clear the passes of St. Jean Pied de Port, and himself followed with a part of the corps by Besnati to Maya, from whence he drove the enemy, and by which we are now in possession of those principal entrances to France. The Light Division, upon returning from the chase of Clausel, followed the route of Hill's corps, which had remained investing the fortress; but upon reaching Trañeta, turned to the left, down the valley of Baztan, where we had been two days, and we expect to remain during the operations carrying on against St. Sebastian.

General Byng's brigade and one of Portuguese of the 2nd (Hill's corps) are now at St. Jean Pied de Tort; Morilla is to his rights the remainder of Hill's force occupy the country about Illesande and Maya. The 7th Division connects us (the Light) with Hill's left, and we in the same manner extend to St. Estevan, and communicate with Graham's corps, whose headquarters I believe are at Hernani, if not Irun. Lord Dalhousie is left in command before Pampeluna, with the 3rd and 4th Divisions, and I understand some Spaniards, with orders to keep it in a state of complete blockade. Fletcher is there, constructing redoubts for the more effectual accomplishment of that object. I think the opinion is general that we shall have it without a siege.

Lord Wellington's headquarters passed through here this morning on their way to Hernani, which place it will reach tomorrow; and from what I can learn, the siege of St. Sebastian is to be undertaken immediately with our best means, and its fall is not questioned in a very short time.

It would appear that our naval support is by no means what we ought to expect; at least so report states, and from good authority too. Our commissariat and ordnance supplies have been delayed in the Tagus by want of convoy, and at this time there is but one ship of war off the coast.

We hear that affairs are looking better in Germany than the armistice gave us reason to expect; if so, our gain here is a good one, and gives a well-grounded hope of accomplishing the great object so long struggled for.

It is needless to say that we have had great difficulties in bringing artillery through the Pyrenees; my troop, however, has accomplished it without sustaining any material injury beyond shaking my wheels, which the halt of a few days gives me time to set right. Two brigades of Portuguese (whose carriages are constructed for this sort of service) and my own, are the only artillery that have yet attempted it.

As I have detained one of the headquarters' people in passing to take this for me, I am obliged to conclude, requesting you to communicate my perfect health to my aunt and sisters, and to

Believe me,

Your very affectionate,

H. D. Ross.

From the 10th to the 14th July the battery remained stationary.

July 15th.—Join the division near Vera. Lord Wellington informs me of my promotion. Headquarters, San Estevan.

July 16th, 17th, and 18th.—Halt. Headquarters, Le Saca.

July 19th, 20th, 21st, and 22nd.—*Do. do.* Batteries opened on the 20th against San Sebastian, consisting of, in all:—On the right, one of two 24-prs. and four 8-inch howitzers; another of two 24-prs. A mortar battery to be established. The above under Major Webber Smith. A third battery of four 24-prs. is under the direction of Major Arricego. The breaching batteries will consist of twelve 24-prs. and four 68-pr. carronades, directed by Colonel Frazer. Colonel Hartmann directs on the left, and has six 18-prs., some 9-prs., and 5½-inch howitzers. The convent and outworks are carried by storm on the 18th.

July 23rd and 24th.—Halt.

July 25th (Sunday).—Sir Rowland Hill attacked and beat at Maya. Generals Byng and Cole forced at Roncesvalles. Lord Wellington at San Sebastian. My troop march in the evening to the bridge of Yanci.

July 26th.—March by Sumbellas Narvarte and Trañeta to Berrueta. Join Sir R. H. Lord Wellington comes up. Headquarters, Madoz.

July 27th (Tuesday).—March towards Lanz, but the road blocked up by Portuguese artillery in the Pass of Valetta. Lord Wellington presses forward to join the 3rd and 4th Divisions in front of Pampeluna, and just arrives in time to occupy a position when attacked by Soult.

July 28th (Wednesday).—Soult again attacks Lord Wellington, but is beaten off four separate times. The 6th Division came up just in time to support Lord Wellington's left. My troop marches to Ollacarez Garten, Sir B. Hill's corps to the heights behind Lazassa.

July 29th (Thursday).—This day spent by the enemy in collecting new force, and reconnaissance and manoeuvres to attack General Hill the next morning. My troop moves to ———.

July 30th (Friday).—Lord Wellington, observing the enemy to have weakened his left, immediately attacks and beats him with the 3rd, 4th, 6th, and 7th Divisions, making great slaughter and taking about 3000 prisoners.

In the meantime Soult had planned an attack on Sir R. Hill, which was executing, and at first with some success; but being shortly after supported by some Spaniards and the Light Division, combined with the disasters which befell Soult's left, put a stop to his efforts, and his whole army retired in some disorder towards Lauz, whither Lord Wellington followed up.

July 31st (Saturday).—Move my troop into this village, Elcarte.

Aug. 3rd (Tuesday).—I set out for Passages to see Colonel Dickson on the subject of procuring new carriages, wheels, &c., who obtains Lord Wellington's permission for my troop to move to this part of the country.

Aug. 7th (Saturday).—Troop arrives at Andonin.

Aug. 11th and 12th.—Land stores at Passages.

Aug. 13th (Friday).—Belson returns from Passages with party, and wheels, stores, &c.

Aug. 19th.—Fleet, with battering train, arrives at Passages.

Aug. 20th (Friday).—Report all my carriages repaired, and troop fit for service."

The following letter, of the date of the last entry, refers to the causes of the failure of the first attack of San Sebastian, the operations which had taken place in the Pyrenees, and the actual situation of the armies:—

To Sir Hew Dalrymple

Andonin, near Ernani,
August 20, 1813.

My dear Sir,

With very sincere thanks, I beg to acknowledge the receipt of your letter of the 7th July, conveying your kind congratulations on my promotion. I likewise request you will do me the favour to offer my hearty acknowledgments to Lady Dalrymple and all the members of your family for their kind wishes on the occasion.

I have great pleasure in hearing that you have been able to collect so large a portion of your household at Delrow this summer, and cannot help feeling a very strong wish to have witnessed the comfort of the happy party, and to have gained the acquaintance of the new members of it. You only wanted the Fanshawes to complete the circle.

We have been long looking with anxious solicitude for the arrival of the reinforcement, and a battering train establishment; the former to secure our position in the Pyrenees—which has in many places been unavoidably too weakly occupied—and for the latter to enable us to recommence the siege of San Sebastian, with a fair prospect of bringing it to a happy conclusion whilst the season is favourable.

You will of course have heard many stories of the cause of the failure of the former attack—and what colour Lord Wellington may have chosen to give it I cannot tell, as we have not yet seen his dispatch, but it is generally understood that he was much disappointed at it, and that he entirely acquits the Artillery and Engineers of any fault. Their share of the work was most effectually done on the 22nd, and there appears to be no doubt that the town would have been carried had the attack been then made; but unfortunately General Oswald, who commanded the 5th Division, being alarmed at the fire which had taken place in some houses immediately behind and close to the breach, represented to Sir T. Graham that the troops would not be able to stand the heat, and in consequence the attempt was given up and the troops withdrawn, after being already in the trenches to go to the assault.

As might be expected, the enemy availed themselves of the time given them to retrench, and the next day another breach was commenced to turn the defences of the former one, and another attack was ordered on the morning of the 25th; but as fortune seems occasionally to run against certain operations, so happened it with this. The signal of assault was made too soon, and the tide was not sufficiently low, and the troops, probably disheartened by the former indecision, got into confusion, and, as I have been told, did not go to work with their usual spirit, and came back in disorder. Many got into the breach—amongst them the officer of Engineers leading the column (Capt. Jones), who was wounded and taken prisoner.

Yesterday the fleet arrived at Passages, having on board the artillery, &c., and the 85th Regiment, with considerable detachments for other regiments, and already the debarkation has commenced. In a few days the batteries will again open, though I fear we shall have to contend with greater difficulties than we ought to have found in the former siege, with the disadvantage of the ardour of the troops being damped.

It is unnecessary for me to say anything of the recent actions in the passes and before Pampeluna, as the official account will long since have reached you. Troops never behaved better than did ours throughout, and the enemy's also showed great perseverance and courage.

My carriages were so completely shaken to pieces that we could not follow back into the passes, and as transport could not be had to send my wheels and other means of refit, I was ordered to this place, in the neighbourhood of Passages, from whence I have got a complete refit, and my troop being reported ready, I am in expectation of an order to rejoin my division in the Pass of Vera.

I have been interrupted by the entrance of James Ross, who, you will be glad to hear, is so much recovered of his wound as to be on the march to rejoin his regiment. He was very unfortunate, in not only losing his baggage and being wounded on the 25th, but being carried to the rear, he was some time at Vittoria without being able to procure money, baggage, or any sort of comfort. In spite of everything he is looking remarkably well, and with the exception of his knee being a little stiff, suffers no inconvenience, and that is wearing off every day.

With regard to the situation of the armies, I can say little more than that they occupy nearly the same ground as before Soult advanced, with this difference, that our troops are differently disposed; the 4th Division being now at La Saca, connecting the Light Division and the Spaniards of Sir T. Graham's corps, and that O'Donnell is now on the heights by Echellur, his former place having been taken by Don Carlos, whose corps now blockades Pampeluna. In addition to the reinforcements from England and Ireland, we have within these few days got the brigade of Guards up from Oporto, looking healthy, and 1500 strong; and we hear the remount for cavalry and artillery has gone to Bilbao.

The report of Lord Aberdeen's departure for the Congress has given the affairs of the north a strong interest here. I hope the cautious policy of Austria will not run too far, and allow Napoleon to give a blow to the Russians and Prussians. We, I trust, shall be able to hold our ground, though I think we must soon expect another effort on the part of Soult to save his fortresses and recover the reputation of his army.

Pray tell Mrs. Ross that James is well, and that he desires to be affectionately remembered to her, as he does likewise to all your family.

The journal contains no entries from the 21st to the 30th August.

Aug. 31st.—The Horse Artillery ordered in the night of the 30th to march immediately to the neighbourhood of Yrun. The enemy make an attack along the line of the Bidassoa, but are beat,

San Sebastian is carried by assault at mid-day, but with severe loss. The enemy retire to the castle, which they hold in strength.

Sir Richard Fletcher is killed, and Sir John Leith and Generals Oswald and Robinson are wounded.

Sept. 4th.—Troop marches back to Andonin.

Sept. 8th.—The batteries open against the castle works at 10 a.m., with sixty pieces of ordnance, and in two hours the governor proposes to surrender.

Sept. 9th.—Garrison lay down their arms in the usual manner, and become prisoners of war.

The following was written to his sister on the 13th September:—

You will be glad to hear of the fall of St. Sebastian, after all the trouble and loss we have had about it. The garrison of the castle surrendered on the 8th, a couple of hours after our batteries opened against it; and yesterday they went through the usual forms and became prisoners of war, to be embarked for England. We have now only to look to the fall of Pampeluna to make us easy in our possession of this frontier, and we are led to suppose it so ill off for provisions that it must soon surrender. We are still ignorant of what is going on in the north of Europe, further than we believe that Austria has declared on the side of the Allies. Upon their success much of our future operations will necessarily depend, and as my prospect of seeing my friends in Scotland rests on our labours here coming to a pause, I am selfish as much as patriotic in wishing the French well beat in all and every part of the globe wherever they are to be found. Norman Ramsay is at present with his troop in this neighbourhood, and we are much together. He is quite well, and bears his unjust treatment and consequent disappointment in the manly and proper way that might be expected of him.

You will no doubt be very much concerned to see the name of Sir Richard Fletcher amongst the fatal list of sufferers in the assault of St. Sebastian. I lament him very much, and feel for his family. He showed much kindness to our dear George, and I have ever esteemed him for it

I had nearly forgotten to tell you that the Prince Regent has been pleased to put me and the other officers who commanded troops and brigades at the Battle of Vittoria on the pension list; that is to say, he has ordered us an addition to our income of five shillings *per diem*. I fear honour and profit are far outrunning my deserts.

The next letter is of the same date, to Sir Hew Dalrymple:—

Andonin,
Sept. 10, 1813.

My dear Sir,

I have much pleasure in acquainting you that the castle of St. Sebastian is in our possession. Our batteries were opened on the morning of the 8th, at ten o'clock, and in less than two hours the garrison offered to surrender. The terms were arranged that day, and yesterday the usual forms were gone through. The prisoners are to keep their private baggage, and General Ney has permission to send an officer with his report to Marshal Soult. They are to be embarked for England as soon as transports are ready to receive them. Their numbers, I understand, are about 1300 effective and nearly 600 wounded and non-competents. We have had the satisfaction, also, to release several officers and 150 men that were taken in the first assault, and in the different sorties of the enemy; amongst the former is Capt. Jones of the Engineers, who was wounded on that occasion, but I am happy to say he is doing well.

I suppose Major Hare has by this time reached London with the account of the successful attack of the town on the 31st, and of the brilliant affairs that took place on that same day in the Pyrenees. I fear very many will feel that the former has been dearly paid for, for our loss has been most severe, and, as in all former sieges, the corps of Engineers has borne a large proportion. You will, I am sure, be much concerned for the death of Sir Richard Fletcher, whose loss will be severely felt by his corps and his friends, for he was an excellent man and a most useful officer. Captains Rhodes and Collyer were young on this service, but were highly spoken of by their corps.

The assault of this place seems to have solved a question that has been long in dispute—whether it is preferable to storm by day or night? which appears to be given decidedly in favour of the former, especially with British troops. Indeed, I am quite sure in this instance the town never could have been carried in the night, and even as it was, difficulties were overcome which by daylight seem almost incredible.

The conduct of the Spaniards under General Freyer, on the 31st, has been particularly gratifying to the army, as it has not been the practice to indulge the Gallician Army with much of our confidence; they have now claimed it of us, for they defended their position most gallantly during the whole day against repeated attacks of a very superior force of the enemy, and several times employed the bayonet.

Soult continues moving about, and it is reported that he is now pointing towards our right, but I don't believe he can for some time make another attempt to relieve Pampeluna; and if he does, we must hope that he will be repelled even better than before, our hands being quit of the care of San Sebastian. With regard to Pampeluna, it is very difficult to form an exact opinion, reports are so various; but I think it is the fashion about head-quarters to say it must soon surrender for want of provisions.

It will give you pleasure to hear that James Ross is about to get on the staff as A.D.C. to General Buchan, who has at length got a brigade of Portuguese. He has turned out a remarkably zealous officer, and as far as his rank will permit, has distinguished himself on all occasions, and is besides highly esteemed by his regiment.

I saw General Bradford lately, when he was looking very well. I have also met Gubbins, who, though looking well, complained of ailing a little; and I fear his ascension above the clouds will not be much in his favour, his regiment having moved into the mountains, which are almost invariably enveloped in clouds or rain.

We have a report brought from the French outposts that the Allies have had some success in the north, but I don't hear that anything certain is known. With us, excepting the departure of Marshal Beresford to Lisbon, I know of nothing worth relating; for we are now grown so old in our positions that we begin to look at our moves backwards and forwards with the same indifference we used to perform them on the Coa and Agueda.

Since our retreat upon Pampeluna no artillery has been taken into the Pass of Vera, and my troop has remained upon the great road leading to Irene, to which place it moved the other day, when Soult attacked on the mountains to the right of it, and since returned here for the benefit of forage and forces.

I must not omit to mention one event of some importance that has occurred to myself—namely, that it has pleased the master general (by order of the prince, we are told) to put me and the other officers who commanded troops and brigades of artillery in the Battle of Vittoria on the Ordnance Pension List for five shillings *per diem*, and the field officers of the corps present on that occasion at the rate of ten shillings.

Will you have the goodness to mention this additional piece of good fortune to my aunt and your own family, to whom I am sure it will give satisfaction; but as the title of pensioner in these times does not increase one's favour with the world, I think we old gentlemen of the artillery ought not to publish our receiving the reward of good service before we may be allowed to have well earned it.

The journal is resumed on the 6th October, the day before the passage of the Bidassoa:—

Oct. 6th.—Receive an order at 5 p.m. to march, so as to assemble at Oyarzun at 2 a.m. on the 7th. March at 10 p.m.

Oct. 7th.—The enemy are attacked in their position on the right bank of the Bidassoa. Our columns (Sir Thomas Graham's corps) move to the attack near Irun at half-past 7 a.m., and in less than two hours the river is crossed by fords only passable at low tide, and the enemy are beat from all their positions, which we occupy, having our piquets near to Urognio.

The 5th Division cross at Fuentarabia; the 1st near the great road of Irun; General Bradford's brigade of Portuguese between these points, and General Wilson's by the fords to the right of the 1st Division. The Spaniards under General Freyer by those in front of San Marcial.

The Light Division at the same time move through Vera, and carry the strong heights in its front and the pass so named, whilst the Spaniards under Generals Longa and Giron attack the heights at the fort and round Monté la Rhune. ("Sir Thomas Graham resigned the command of his corps to Sir John Hope on the evening of the 7th, and sailed for England on the 10th October.")

Oct. 8th.—The enemy still hold the rocky summit of Monté la Rhune, but in the evening the Spaniards, by driving them from some heights near it, so threaten to cut off their retreat that they withdraw in the night.

Oct. 9th.—Monté la Rhune occupied by the Spaniards. My troop is ordered to Oyarzun.

The same day he writes to Sir Hew Dalrymple:—

Camp, Irun,
October 9, 1813.

My dear Sir,

I have much pleasure in telling you that the army crossed the Bidassoa on the morning of the 7th, and that it now holds footing in France.

Our columns of attack were put in motion about half-past seven o'clock, and I think in less than two hours we had full possession of the whole of the enemy's position, which was remarkably strong, but most shamefully defended.

Our army passed the river by many fords, but which are only practicable at low tide—I believe in all amounting to seven or eight. The 5th Division passed by those at Fuentarabia, ascending the opposite heights, and driving the enemy before them along the ridges near the coast. The 1st Division, Bradford's and Wilson's Portuguese Brigades, at the same time crossed by the fords near the great road from Irun; and the Spaniards under General Freyer moved forward by those immediately in front of the ground they have so long defended, and attacking the enemy with the most steady and determined bearing, drove them from ground that appeared almost inaccessible.

Whilst these corps gained their point, the Light and 4th Divisions were equally successful in carrying the strong ground in the Pass of Vera, and General Giron, with the Spanish reserve, moved upon their right upon the Monté la Rhune, which is quite inaccessible to assault, and which the enemy still held last night. Today I understand Lord Wellington is moving a considerable force round its right, with the view to compel them to abandon it.

Demonstrations were also to be made by our forces at Maya and Roncesvalles, but what has been done there I have not heard. Our troops as usual behaved most gallantly, and the Spaniards really conducted themselves as well as could be wished. Our loss is very trifling, and that of the enemy cannot be much greater, for when once forced they retired even quicker than usual, leaving the artillery they had in position, to the amount of ten or twelve pieces; and I believe we have but few prisoners besides the wounded.

Soult is said to have left the army for the north on the 5th or 6th, and the prisoners say that Suchet arrived at Bayonne to succeed him in command on the evening of the 6th inst. They all agree that our attack was quite unexpected; and really the arrangements for it were so secretly and suddenly effected that it probably was so.

If we succeed in getting Monté la Rhune our position will be greatly improved, and the entrances into France will be well opened to us.

The cavalry and artillery, as in the former actions, have had little to do in this business. My troop moves back tomorrow to Oyarzun, and the brigades belonging to the 3rd and 4th Division, which were also following up on this road, are halted; and I understand we are for the present to remain on the Tolosa road, in case we should be required to join our divisions more to the right; though I hope the early fall of Pampeluna will prevent the enemy making any offensive show in that direction, both because the country is beyond description bad for artillery, and as I hope we shall meet with no serious obstruction to a further advance into France.

Sir Thomas Graham resigned his command to Sir John Hope in the evening of the 7th, after the fight ended, and is, I understand, to embark for England today or tomorrow. It is a singular piece of good fortune for him to have seen the allied army enter the enemy's country before his departure.

The next letter will be found one of great interest, in reference to the cause of failure in the first assault on San Sebastian, and the causes which had led to the many heavy losses of Engineer officers on this and other occasions. The letters which follow refer to the battle of the Nivelle on the 10th November—an occasion on which Lieut.-Colonel Ross's battery specially distinguished itself—the passage of the Nive on the 9th December, and the battle fought near Bayonne on the 13th December.

To Sir Hew Dalrymple

Headquarters, Vera,
October 31, 1813.

My dear Sir,

Ever since my letter of the 9th inst. we have daily expected an event which I then mentioned as probable, but which has not yet taken place—I mean the surrender of Pampeluna, upon which our forward operations seem entirely to depend. The governor has husbanded his means far beyond what could have been expected; for although he was known early in September to have been under the necessity of using horseflesh and a reduced ration of bread, he still demands terms the most unreasonable, and such as cannot be granted.

Colonel Goldfinch of the Engineers, who has all along been with Don Carlos assisting in the blockade, reports that a negotiation was opened by the governor sending out his chief of the staff (I think on the 25th), but his proposals were so absurd that they were declared inadmissible, and the treaty was broken off. They were no less than requiring to be allowed the honours of war, and to march his garrison, with six or eight pieces of field artillery, into France, upon parole of honour not to serve for twelve months.

Since then some communications have passed, but no adjustment has as yet taken place; and though there cannot be a doubt as to the wretched state of the garrison and its inhabitants, yet the firmness of the governor would seem still to put our hopes of possession at an uncertain date.

Intercepted letters, as well as other information, appeared to place it beyond the power of chance that it could hold out after the 28th; and Lord Wellington, acting upon this, made arrangements to attack along the whole line of Soult's position. Unfortunately, however, the governor's obstinacy and the inclemency of the weather has marred our hopes, and instead of enjoying comfortable quarters which we expected in France, we are still shivering in the mountains.

Preparatory to the intended attack, my troop and two brigades of 9-prs. were moved here from the neighbourhood of Oyarzun, to be ready to act with the left centre column in the direction of Sarre; and a most severe march we had of it, owing to the badness of the weather and to the intricacy and badness of the road. Even should Pampeluna fall, at present I fear we could not take immediate advantage of it to advance, as the country is so inundated and the roads cut up by incessant rain, that I know that our movements would be dreadfully embarrassed. The rain commenced in the night of the 26th (that on which I marched), and has continued ever since with very little intermission.

I believe I mentioned in my last that Soult had left the army in our front, and had been succeeded in command by Suchet. It is a curious circumstance that this report, unfounded as it was, should for some time have been generally credited throughout the army, and that it should have been also the general belief in that of the enemy, from whence it came.

I have to thank you for a letter of the 28th September, which was brought me about ten days ago. In it you speak of the assault of San Sebastian, and mention a whisper being abroad that some of the troops did not perform their part so well as they ought. In this observation I suppose you allude to the first assault (which most assuredly failed on that account), and not to the last and successful one, regarding which I have never heard the gallantry of any corps questioned. Indeed, had their discipline afterwards, when in possession of the town, been equal to their conduct in carrying it, every individual concerned would have deserved a more than common fame; for greater difficulties were never overcome or more bravery shown by any troops than was displayed in the storm.

Unfortunately, it was far otherwise on the first attempt, and I feel no delicacy in stating what the whole army declare, that the place ought to have been ours had the directing general possessed more energy on the occasion. From all I can learn, the case was exactly this:— The assault was to be made at daybreak, and to commence by signal from Sir Richard Fletcher. Some say the signal was given (and possibly it might be so) too soon; the troops, however, went on, and Captain Jones of the Engineers, followed by the greater part of the grenadiers of the Royals, carried the breach and entered the place. Support, however, hung back, and the reason assigned for it is publicly talked of to be this: that General Oswald—who was directing the attack, and at the head of the trench—called out at an unlucky moment to Sir Thomas Graham, who stood a little way from him, 'It won't do, it won't do; shall we call them back?' or some words to that effect, which naturally being overheard by all near, checked ardour, and lost the time which ought to have been taken advantage of whilst the enemy was alarmed and the breach in our possession.

Jones, I am well acquainted with, and on his being released (for he was wounded and taken after entering the place) by the surrender of the castle, assured me that had the support followed him the place was carried; for the enemy had fled from the breach and were abandoning the adjoining ramparts, when, finding how matters stood without, they rallied, and he was wounded on the breach, having returned to call on and direct the column, which never approached him.

The only answer I can give to the question respecting the extravagant and ill-judged employment of Engineer officers to lead the forlorn hope in all storming parties with this army, is what appears but too true—that the infantry officer, in general, is ignorant of the terms and construction of the works to be carried, and when he undertakes to lead his men, generally bargains for a director, which the high spirit and ardent zeal of the Engineers too greedily seize upon as an opportunity of signalising themselves, and which I fear the commanding officer of Engineers has rather encouraged than resisted.

Whatever the cause may be that has gained the custom such general use, all must agree that it is one much to be deplored, and cannot too soon be put a stop to; indeed, I have heard it much talked of in the army, but I think I have generally heard it defended by the officers of Engineers themselves.

To Sir Hew Dalrymple

Camp in front of St. Ré (*sic*)

November 12, 1813.

My dear Sir,

It is with much pleasure I have again to mention our success in the attack of the enemy's position on the 10th inst., and though I fear we have to lament the loss of many valuable officers and a considerable number of men, yet from all I can learn it will turn out to be less than might have been expected, from the natural and artificial strength of the country over which we had to fight. I cannot venture to describe either the country or the movements of our different columns, the former being so mountainous that one could observe little more than what occurred with his own.

My letter of the 31st *ultimo* told you that my troop and two 9-pr. brigades had been moved into the Pass of Vera, preparatory to the attack (which but for the weather was to have taken place sooner than it did), where we remained till the morning of the 10th, when we moved with the 4th Division against the village of Sarre and the strong redoubts the enemy had constructed on all the heights round it. These we soon carried, whilst the Light Division moved down from La Rhune and stormed the lesser mountain of that name, which the enemy had entrenched and occupied in force. The 7th and 3rd Divisions were on our right, and, with the 4th, composed the right centre column under Sir William Beresford. These divisions were the only part of the army that came under my observation, and all appeared to move admirably, driving the enemy successively from all their redoubts; and before mid-day we had carried their last position, which I can only designate by the heights of Ascani, which were very strong, and upon which the enemy had a second line of redoubts, all of which they were compelled to abandon, and in one our advance was so rapid that the garrison, consisting of 500 men, were shut in and obliged to lay down their arms.

The right column was under Sir Rowland Hill, and composed of his own corps and the 6th Division. He moved from Maya, attacking and turning the left of the enemy's position, which we hear was well executed, for at noon he had gained the mountains on the right of the Nivelle, whilst the right centre crossed the river at St. Ré, (sic), after driving the enemy from its right bank, where he seemed anxious to make a stand; but the 3rd and 7th Divisions, supported by my troop, soon drove them from it, and at night our right and right centre column took up their ground, extending from the Nivelle towards the Pyrenees in the direction of Mondarin.

The left centre, which was composed of the 2nd Division and the Spaniards, under Sir John Hope, remained under the left bank of the Nivelle, from Ascani towards St. Jean de Luz, which place the enemy abandoned in the night, and last night we could see them at Bidart, when they were slightly engaged with the advance of Sir John Hope's column, which crossed the Nivelle yesterday morning, as did likewise the left centre column.

We have today been in expectation of an order to advance, but as yet it has not arrived. From what I can discover, it is not likely that we shall carry our advance much farther into France; but opinion seems divided whether the Nive or the Adour will be the line we shall take up, and I think there is no doubt that we can do which we please, for the spirit of the French Army is too low to give us a hope of its committing itself by risking a general action.

It is not in my power to add much more to this, nor can I write to my sisters, I therefore beg you will send it to them, or communicate to them my perfect safety and sound health; and it may also be a satisfaction to them to hear that we are not likely to have any more fighting for our quarters, and that as soon as I find the army at rest I mean to ask leave of absence.

You will be sorry to hear that Barnard has got a severe wound, but whether it is considered dangerous or not I have not been able to learn; I most sincerely hope it is not. Of my relations in Sir Rowland Hill's corps I have no account, nor have I heard anything of Sir John Hope's loss; and as the brunt of the action seemed to fall on the centre columns, I should hope neither suffered much. My troop was more unfortunate than it has usually been, having one man killed and one officer and ten men wounded; but I am happy to say that the latter promise to do well.

I have to thank you for a joint letter from my aunt and yourself, dated the 21st, which reached me a few days ago.

We have been cheered in our advance by the confirmation of the disasters that have befallen Buonaparte in the north, which are well known to the inhabitants and the French Army. I am sorry to say our disorderly Spanish allies have already given evidence of the little hope we have of conciliating the inhabitants; who otherwise seem well disposed to us.

Every exertion is making to enforce order, and I hope it will be attended with success. My kindest affection to all friends, and

Believe me, my dear Sir,

Your faithful and affectionate,

H. D. R.

To Sir Hew Dalrymple

St. Pé,
December 6, 1813.

My dear Sir,

Since I wrote to Mrs. Ross last week, she will have told you of my application for leave of absence, with the suspense attending it. This still continues, for as yet I have had no communication from the adjutant-general on this subject, and the weather has been so bad and the roads so much cut up that for the last week it has been barely possible for those who are obliged to travel, or for those who can avoid it, to cross the threshold of his door. I have therefore been a close prisoner to my quarter, and until the return of my messenger tomorrow from headquarters, I shall remain ignorant if I have any better prospect of success.

I cannot but feel it a disappointment being detained here at present; for from what I have seen of the country, and what the inhabitants say of the climate at this season, I should imagine a complete bar is put to our advancing for some time, and it is easy to foresee that the delay I at present suffer will curtail my stay at home hereafter, should I succeed in getting there at last.

Grant, you will know is gone home (I hear) very ill, and from his brigade being instantly given to Vivian, I should guess he has no immediate intention to return. I know he is disappointed in not being named a brigadier in this army, which he was led to expect on coming out, as well as to hold the hussar brigade.

The general order you mention as having seen in a Spanish paper is genuine, and was occasioned by the irregularity of some of the 1st Division when entering Urogne (I believe the Light Company of the Guards and Light Germans) on the 7th October; and the cause of the threat held out to the officers, I understand, was well deserved (but has not been put in force), no effort having been made by them to restrain their men when breaking their ranks for plunder, contrary to a particular order recently given, and absolutely in the very face of the enemy.

To Sir Hew Dalrymple

Villa Franque,
December 14, 1813.

My dear Sir,

I am happy in having again to communicate the agreeable intelligence of our continued success in beating the enemy. On the 8th inst. I was ordered to place myself under the orders of Sir Rowland Hill, and to remain with his corps, for which purpose I marched to La Resson, where the following morning I covered General Pringle's and General Buchan's brigades in forcing the fords opposite that place. The rest of Sir Rowland Hill's corps passed the Nive at Combo, and Marshal Beresford brought the 5th Division across at Usturitz, and at every place the fords were carried with a very trifling loss, and the enemy driven along the heights over which runs the great road from St. Jean Pied de Port to Bayonne.

The armies halted in front of each other in position about a league from Bayonne at dark, to which time firing continued; and at night the enemy withdrew into his entrenched camp on this side, and passing a great part of his army through Bayonne, attacked our left on the other side of the Nive the following morning; but I only know what took place there by report, and a very distant view. I shall therefore only say that he had no reason to boast of any advantage on that or the two following days, when he tried his fortune against that part of our army; and I hear everyone speaks favourably of the conduct of our troops.

On the evening of the 12th we observed him bringing troops back from the left of the Nive into Bayonne, and from that side during the night he withdrew altogether, leaving only a force to hold his entrenchments, which are very strong, and at daylight presented nearly his whole army in front of Sir Rowland Hill's position, which was so thinly occupied (having only his own corps to occupy the whole extent from the Adour to the Nive, the 6th Division having gone back on the 10th to support the left when attacked) that had the conduct of his troops been what it ought, or that of ours less glorious, our situation would have been perilous.

But through the good nerve of Sir Rowland, seconded by the gallantry of the generals and troops, all the enemy's attacks were repulsed with a most severe loss; and although repeated four several times to the very point of our position before any support could come across to us (owing to the horrid state of the roads, particularly near the river), he was in all forced back at the point of the bayonet, and suffered a dreadful carnage by our fire both in his advance and retreat.

Today he seems quite satisfied with what he has met with on this side, and as Lord Wellington brought over the 6th and 3rd Divisions to us just as his fourth attack failed, and which probably deterred him from another trial, I think he will not again look at us. On the other side we are, I am told, constructing some strong redoubts to strengthen our line, and I suppose the same will be done here; and in the meantime we have placed our right close to the banks of the Adour, so as to intercept the navigation, from which I understand Lord Wellington hopes to straiten the army for provisions, as it is known the chief supply is brought from the interior by water carriage.

I am obliged to close this in haste, and have it only in my power to beg my sisters may be told that I am quite well.

To Mrs. Ross
Villa Franque, near Bayonne
December 19, 1813.

My dear Aunt,

Since my last letter to you the prospect I then had of visiting England this winter has nearly vanished, but for this change no doubt the *Times* will have prepared you; and as you will have received Lord Wellington's despatch before this can have reached you, you will see that we have little chance of quiet for putting the army into winter quarters, and consequently I cannot think of pressing my application for leave of absence. Our defeat of Soult's attack was the most splendid thing I have ever seen, and I understand Lord Wellington has declared his intention of marking with his particular approbation the conduct of Sir Rowland Hill and his corps on the 13th in his report to government

I wrote to Sir Hew the other day a few hasty lines, in the hope of sending it by Major Hill, who takes home the despatch, which I hope he will get soon. I had not then, nor have I now, sufficient time to say much on the subject of our work on the 13th, but I am sure you will be glad to hear that I have received the handsomest acknowledgments from Sir Rowland Hill and Sir William Stewart for the services of my troop on the 13th. The former sent for me to say that we had rendered him such services that, besides thanks, he wished to give a stronger mark of approbation by recommending one of my officers for promotion, and he has sent in the name of Major Jenkinson, who I hope will get his lieut.-colonelcy.

We are now making our position so strong (and having more troops to occupy it) that I don't think there is the most distant chance of Soult's looking at us again; and as the cavalry are all coming up and moving to our right, it is probable we shall completely shut him into Bayonne on this side the Adour, and take up our line on that river, which will give us possession of a great deal of fine country and plenty of forage, and possibly, by shutting the navigation of the river, compel the enemy's army to retire from it.

A few additional details of the operations from the 10th November to the end of the year, are given in the journal:—

Nov. 10th.—The army, being in four columns (the right, Hill's corps and 6th Division at Maya, under Sir Rowland; the right centre, the 3rd, 4th, and 7th Divisions at Zugarramurdi, Eshela, and Pass of Sarre, under Marshal Beresford; the left centre, General Heron's Spaniards, by the right of La Rhune, and Light Division over La Rhune, under General Alten; the left being General Freyre's Spaniards and Sir John Hope's corps, under Sir John), moved at daybreak to attack the enemy, and before mid-day beat them from all their positions. My troop lost one man (Gunner Thompson) killed, Lieut. Day, Serjeant Unsworth, Corporal Morgan, and nine gunners wounded. Halt at St. Pé.

Nov. 23rd (Tuesday).—The Light Division drive in the enemy's outposts, and establish their picquets near to Bayonne.

Dec 7th (Tuesday)—Receive an order from Sir George Murray to march the next day, to place my troop under the orders of Sir Rowland Hill.

Dec 8th (Wednesday).—March by Espaletti to La Risson.

Dec 9th. (Thursday)—Cover the passage of the ford of La Rissoa by the brigades of General Pringle and General Buchan at daybreak. Sir Rowland Hill, with the rest of his corps, force the passage of the

Nive about the same time, under the fire of Colonel Tulloch's artillery at Cambo. Sir Henry Clinton also passes at Asturitz. Each corps covers the heights on the right of the Nive, and driving the enemy at all points, assemble on the great road from Bayonne to St. Jean Pied de Port, about a league from the former place, where we find the enemy in position, and it being too late to attack him, we are put in position opposite to him, but a cannonade and fire of musketry is kept up until dark.

Dec 10th (Friday).—The enemy having retired into their entrenched camp, we move on to the village of St. Pierre, where we take up a position about two miles from Bayonne.

Dec 11th (Saturday).—During the preceding night the enemy moved the chief of their army through Bayonne to the left of the Nive, and at daybreak attack and drive in the picquets of the 2nd and 5th Divisions, and follow up their advantage in force until brought up by the Light Division formed at Arcangues, and the 1st coming up to support the 8th in front of Bidart.

Dec 12th (Sunday).—The enemy continue their attack on the left, but without making any great impression.

Dec 13th (Monday).—In the night the enemy drew their army from the left to the right of the Nive, and at daylight their columns are seen ready to move to the attack of Sir Rowland Hill's corps, which alone occupied a position from the Adour to the Nive, passing in front of La Grande Mouguerre and Villa Franque, and having the village of St. Pierre for its centre (the 6th Division had crossed to the left when the attack was made on that side). Fortunately the enemy did not commence his attack until about eight o'clock, which gave Sir Rowland time to make his dispositions, and enabled him to recall General Barnes' brigade (which had marched to observe some movements of their cavalry in our rear), and also to bring up the Portuguese division quartered in Villa Franque.

The principal attack was directed against the village of St. Pierre, on the main road, and the continuation of the ridge of hills on which it stands to the left of it. Four times they advanced their columns close up, though under a most destructive fire of artillery, and as often were driven back with great slaughter. The brunt of the action fell on General Barnes' brigade, at the village, which lost 47 men, and the General wounded. At this point Day's two guns were posted, and lost five men wounded, besides Trumpeter Burnett killed.

Jenkinson's division of guns were to the left of the village, and suffered no loss except his own horse wounded in two places. Belson was absent with his division at Assuna, with Col. Vivian's Brigade. My own horse was killed. The men wounded were gunners Morgan, Slater, Greaves, Yeates, and Francis Clayton.

The next entry records the receipt of leave of absence to England:—

Jan. 1st, 1814.—Receive a letter from Colonel Dickson informing me that Lord Wellington had given me two months leave from the 7th inst.

Jan. 2nd.—Give over the charge of my troop to Jenkinson, and set out for headquarters, Dine with Dickson.

On the 7th he sailed from Passages for Falmouth, where he arrived on the 17th, and found himself unable to proceed owing to the roads being blocked with snow.

Jan. 18th.—With difficulty get to Truro.

Jan. 19th.—On horseback to Bodmin.

Jan. 20th.—To Liskeard.

Jan. 21st.—To Plymouth.

Jan. 22nd.—Stay at *Ditto.*

Jan. 23rd.—In chaise (four horses) to Ivybridge, and afterwards on horseback to Exeter.

Jan. 24th.—To Taunton. Chaise, four horses.

Jan. 25th.—To Chippenham. *Do.*

Jan. 26th.—To London. *Do.*

Feb. 15th.—Leave London for Edinburgh in the mail.

Feb. 18th.—Arrive in Edinburgh.

The gratifying letter which follows was addressed by Lieut.-General the Hon. Sir William Stewart (afterwards Marquis of Londonderry) to Major Jenkinson, Colonel Ross's Second Captain and intimate friend, after he had sailed for England:—

Near Petit Mongueres,
January 18, 1814.

My dear Sir,

The official reports which Sir Rowland Hill and I had the honour of transmitting to the Commander of the Forces after the action of the 13th December not having been made public by His Excellency, Sir Rowland and I are apprehensive that the high approbation which we most justly entertained for the eminent services of all under our orders in that action has not appeared so manifest to the gallant commanders and their corps as both our feelings and our duty point out that it ought to have been.

Under this impression I embrace the present opportunity of enclosing for your perusal, and for you to communicate to Lieut.-Colonel Ross when conveniently in your power, a copy of my official letter to Sir Rowland Hill, of the 14th December, and likewise a copy of that lieut.-general's to the Marquess of Wellington upon the same subject.

By a reference to these documents Lieut.-Colonel Ross and you will perceive the estimation which was most justly felt by Sir Rowland and myself for the services of your Horse Brigade in the action of the 13th *ultimo*.

I have the honour, furthermore, of stating that, in consequence of your own personal exertions and distinguished gallantry during the part of the combat when you were detached under my more special direction with part of Lt.-Col. Ross's Brigade, I executed the pleasing duty of submitting your name to the Commander of the Forces, through Sir Rowland Hill, for brevet promotion.

I have the honour to be, with regard,
Your faithful servant,
(Signed)   W. Stewart.
L.-G.

Major Jenkinson,
R.H.A.

The following letter from Major Jenkinson contains an excellent account of the operations at the period of the passage of the Adour and the Battle of Orthez, ending with the reception of Lord Wellington at Bordeaux, and carries on the service of the Chestnut Troop after Lieut.-Colonel Ross's departure:—

My dear Ross,

Little did I think when I last wrote to you that we should so soon have reached the Adour, and that after a general action as interesting, as decisive, and important as any which you had the good fortune to see.

It will be amusing to you to follow our movements on the map, and to peruse the details of operations which have led to such rapid, such unexpected, and such glorious results.

One of these was what I before mentioned to you to be in contemplation—the crossing the Adour at its mouth—and the preparations for which will ever be memorable proofs of the great mind and genius of our commander. For this purpose boats of enormous dimensions had long been collecting at St. Jean de Luz, with cables and anchors of no ordinary size, and every other preparation made for so stupendous an undertaking—one which would have appalled most men, and which I humbly conceive could not have been accomplished but with the aid of our naval skill and superiority.

Not only was there wind and a most rapid stream to calculate against, but there was a frigate and fortified town possessing all the means of annoyance and destruction that could be devised; to counteract which, however, two booms were prepared, composed of masts of ships linked together by massive chains, made fast to 18-prs. on either shore, and moored up and down the stream by very large anchors and cables. The boats of the bridge are also moored fore and aft, and made fast to either shore in a similar way.

Previous to the commencement of this operation, the blockade of Bayonne between the Adour and Nive had been taken up by the 5th Division, and that between the Nive and the sea by Spaniards; the remaining parts of Sir John Hope's corps being concentrated near the mouth of the Adour, and left disposable.

When the weather permitted the fleet put to sea, and reached the mouth of the river in the evening. It did not, however, get in until the next day, nor without being threatened with destruction when crossing the bar, where all agree in terming the surf the most awful and dangerous ever seen; and when they did enter, it occupied them three days to dress their boats, for such was the rapidity of the stream that they could only work at slack tide.

To cover this operation, Morrison's 18-prs. had been placed in battery on the left bank, and four hundred of the Guards, with some rockets, passed over to the light bank. As soon as the enemy discovered that, they made a sortie from the citadel, and would probably have overpowered our small force had not one of the rockets of the first discharge penetrated into the centre of their column, which so paralysed them as to make many of them throw away their arms and disperse, leaving several of them most horribly burnt. The bridge was then completed in tranquillity, Sir John Hope's corps passed over, St. Etienne taken by storm, and the citadel invested.

Not less difficult was our task, as you will easily conceive from your recollection of the country and its state—for we had the Arran, the Bidouza, the Oleron, and the Pau Rivers to cross before it became a question whether we could or not pass the Adour, and that in the face of a force at least equal if not superior to ours.

Sir Rowland Hill's corps, the 3rd, 4th, 6th, 7th, and Light Divisions, were then assembled, and the former directed to turn the Arran while the latter threatened the enemy's front, which compelled Soult to retire behind the Bidouza, posting in front of St. Palais about 8000 men, in a most favourable position for covering it which there presented itself.

This post Lord Wellington directed Sir Rowland Hill to dispossess the enemy of immediately, which was done, but not without an obstinate resistance, for they were preparing the bridges for destruction, in which, however, they failed, and those important passes over the Bidouza River were preserved almost entire. Soult then withdrew his army to the right bank of the Oleron, covering his front with that river, placing his right upon the Adour and his left at Sanveterre, where the ground was very strong and presented a most favourable *appui*.

The left bank of the Oleron was then occupied by the 3rd and 4th Divisions, and the further operations suspended until the 6th and 7th Divisions were closed up to support them, and the Light Division to that of Sir Rowland Hill; every preparation being made in the meantime to induce the enemy to suppose that it was our intention to force the passage of the river.

On the morning of the 24th of February the enemy was still in position, and it was known that his whole force was then assembled; it therefore became necessary again to turn him, for which purpose the Light Division, supported by Sir Rowland Hill's corps, had been ordered to pass the Gave de Mauleon at Navas and assemble at Villeneuve, where we found no enemy to oppose our passage of the Oleron, which after removing the obstacles placed in our way we forded, and before four o'clock in the evening were placed in the Orthez road, in rear of the enemy's right.

During the night our pontoon bridge was laid, and on the morning of the 25th the enemy was seen retiring in all directions, and as soon as Lord Wellington arrived our whole army was put in motion, our column being, as usual, led by his lordship. We reached the very commanding heights about Orthez about mid-day, when the enemy made a very ineffectual attempt to destroy the bridge over the Pau, and were in such confusion in the town as can only be properly known to one who witnessed that of Vittoria.

Lord Wellington immediately ordered up your troop, which quickly crowned the height, and acquitted itself, as you so well know it always does, to the satisfaction of every person. Their rapid and well-directed fire soon dispersed the enemy's masses of infantry and cavalry, and increased their confusion beyond all conception; but they had so barricaded the bridge and occupied so strongly the houses which commanded it, that it would have been almost impossible to force it; the army was therefore placed in cantonments on the left bank of the Pau.

On the 26th the dispositions were made for crossing the Pau, Sir William Beresford being directed to pass it wherever he might discover fords; the 6th Division held in readiness to force the bridge of Orthez; Sir Rowland Hill's corps and the Light Division the fords above that place.

In the interim Sir Thomas Picton discovered and passed a ford at Berens, below Orthez, and we were desired to make a flank movement with the 6th Division to support him, Sir Rowland Hill's corps being left to take our ground and observe the enemy's movements.

On the morning of the 27th, the 3rd, 4th, 6th, 7th, and Light Divisions of Infantry, Lord Ed. Somerset and Colonel Vivian's brigades of cavalry, yours and Colonel Gardiner's troops of Horse Artillery, Maxwell's, Turner's, Michell's, and Sympher's brigades were across the river, and our pontoon bridge established at Berens. The enemy was soon perceived to be in position, with his right on St. Boés and his left on Orthez and covering the fords above it, his centre being crowded with columns of infantry in echelon, which gave to his position a formidable and appalling appearance.

Lord Wellington's dispositions were soon made, and the 4th Division, supported by the 7th, directed to attack and turn the enemy's light, whilst the Light, 3rd, and 6th Divisions should menace his centre. Sir Rowland Hill was ordered to force the passage of the river where he could put himself in communication with us, and push on on the only road which the enemy had to retire upon.

The attack commenced about ten o'clock upon the village of St. Boés, where the contest was most severe but never doubtful, and as soon as we were firmly possessed of it the other divisions advanced, and the action became general along the whole line, the enemy making such a resistance as I have never before seen. The fierce and rapid onset, however, of all our columns it was evident made them waver, and about one o'clock they began to give way; at first withdrawing with some order, but when closely pursued by us, converting that into a disgraceful and disorderly flight, leaving their artillery and throwing away their arms, and alone consulting their individual safety.

As soon as the ground would admit of it, the artillery began to debouche, and three times was your troop and Gardiner's and Sympher's brigade in line, keeping up a destructive and most dreadful fire upon the enemy's retiring columns; and you will believe, my dear Ross, what a proud moment it was for me to find myself in a general action, in the command of such fine fellows as you know yours to be. Lord Wellington kept us by him the whole day, and either communicated his orders in person to me or sent an *aide-de-camp*.

To tell you of the subsequent disorderly flights of the enemy, of the dispersion of their rear-guard by General Barnes at Aire, of our tranquil passage of the Adour, of the capture of their immense magazine at Dax and Mont de Marçan, is but to tell you how brilliant a victory we have gained, which the present positions of our army enhance and confirm, even had it no such important result as the occupation of this superb and magnificent city, and its spontaneous declaration in favour of its legitimate sovereign.

Bordeaux, March 13th, 1814.—On the 12th of March—a memorable day, in truth, should it prove to be that of the restoration of the Bourbons—we moved towards this place with Colonel Vivian's brigade of cavalry and the 7th Division under Marshal Beresford's command, and when within two miles of it we halted to close up and refresh the column, when the marshal put himself at its head to make his public entry into the city.

About one mile from it the mayor, with a mounted retinue in their full dress, met the marshal, and after the usual salutes and ceremonies, he drew a paper from his pocket, which he read in a very audible voice, expressing on the part of the inhabitants the pleasure they felt at the approach of those who might be so justly termed the saviours and deliverers of the world. He came also, he said, to solicit the Marshal's permission to hoist the white flag, and to allow the inhabitants of Bordeaux to declare for their legitimate sovereign, Louis XVIII., at the first mention of which the air was rent with cries of '*Vive le Roi*,' '*Vive les braves et généreux Anglais.*'

As soon as silence could be obtained, he continued to state that for twenty-five years the Bordelais had suffered under the most galling tyranny and oppression, which had reduced their once most flourishing city to a state which no one could envy. 'Long,' said he, 'have we wished for this moment, when the people could without restraint declare their opinions.' They then formally took from their hats and waists their tri-coloured sashes and cockades, and substituted the white ones, when there was such a shout of loyalty as beggars all description; and I am persuaded that I speak within bounds when I state there were 50,000 spectators of this most interesting event.

The marshal then replied, and said that the motives and views of the English Government were too well known to require any professions on his part. The English troops did not come to force the inhabitants of Bordeaux to declare for one person or another, and he trusted that they had well weighed the consequences of failure before they had made their declaration in favour of Louis XVIII., and having done so, that they were ready and determined to support it.

If the opinions and wishes all seemed to express were the spontaneous declarations of the people, the English could not but wish that so good a cause might be successful; but he begged to inform them that we did not wish to be considered as principals, whatever aid we might give. The act was their own, and from them it must derive its best support.

This reply was frequently interrupted with the cries, '*Vive le Roi*,' '*Vive les Anglais*,' and after it we were conducted by the Mayor to the Commune, where all the municipality, in full dress, were assembled to receive us. Again did the marshal fully explain the motives and views of the English Government, and again express a hope that no false promises had been held out to the people to make them take the step they had done; the reply to which was made by a deputation bearing the white flag, and requesting to hoist it in the name of the people.

Two hours after this interesting scene the Duc d'Angoulême arrived, but any attempt to describe the manner in which he was received would be ridiculous, as also his reception at the theatre the night after, the very lobby being so crowded as to make it difficult to move; and it was very evident the people came to see the Duc d'Angoulême, and not the play.

Lieut.-Colonel Ross's services in the Peninsular campaigns were rewarded in 1815 by his being created a Knight Commander of the Bath and a Knight of the Tower and Sword of Portugal.

The peace of 1814 led to the return of the Chestnut Troop from the south of France, and he rejoined it at Warley. The following letter, written the day before his march for the Waterloo campaign, is the last of the series to Sir Hew Dalrymple in the possession of Sir Hew Ross's family:—

Woolwich,
May 26, 1815.

My dear Sir,

On looking over my papers in the course of packing up, I have found the enclosed, which you were good enough to say you would like to have, and which I long since intended to have sent you. (Referring to his record of services, which will be found at the end of this memoir.) I feel myself much obliged by your wish, and much gratified by your thinking my story worth preserving. I have, after hard fighting and much complaint, succeeded in getting my troop better made up than I at first expected, though it is still very far from what I could wish. My officers, however, are excellent, and through their exertions and willing attention I still flatter myself that we shall maintain our reputation through the ensuing campaign

I find only two troops are to be attached to cavalry (Gardiner's and Smith's to the two hussar brigades), the rest are to be in reserve.

I will, however, trouble you from time to time with an account of our proceedings, and you shall hear from me so soon as I meet Leighton.

Sir Hew's journal of this campaign is very brief and concise:—

Warley, May 10th, 1815.—Receive an order to march to Woolwich, to fit for service.

May 27th.—March to Chatham.

May 28th.—To Canterbury.

May 29th.—Halt.

May 30th.—To Ramsgate, and embark on board without accident by one o'clock p.m., and sail at five.

May 31st.—Convoy off Ostend at daybreak, but the tide being out, lay off the harbour till six p.m. Three subdivisions land and march to Saas.

June 1st.—The remainder disembark at daylight.

June 2nd.—Halt.

June 3rd.—March to Bruges.

June 4th.—To Eccloo.

June 5th.—Through Ghent to Oostaker, four miles beyond.

June 7th.—Troop inspected by Sir George Wood and Frazer. I accompany them to Bruxelles. Go to a ball at the Duke of Wellington's.

June 10th.—Return to Oostaker.

June 12th.—March through Alost to Meloart. Go with Ramsay and Parker to see an inspection of the Horse Artillery at Welle, consisting of "E," "F," "G," "I," and "H" Troops, and Whinyates' Rocket Troop. We afterwards call on Lord Uxbridge at Ninove, and dine with Macdonald at Oordeghem.

June 13th.—March to Perk, where we occupy quarters, part of the troop lying at ——.

June 15th.—Dine with Sir James Kempt at Brussels. Return to Perk at night, in consequence of some of the troops being put in motion, the enemy being reported to have attacked the Prussians.

June 16th.—At seven p.m. receive an order to march through Brussels, there to join the reserve. Headquarters moved to Waterloo.

The enemy attack the 5th Division under Sir Thomas Picton, and are repulsed.

June 17th.—Having continued our march during the night, at daybreak Major Drummond received an order for the reserve to proceed towards Genappe; at which place, having just arrived, we meet the whole army falling back on the position in front of Waterloo, to which we retire.

June 18th.—The army is placed in position, and at half-past ten a.m. I am ordered to move my troop to the heights on the right of the *chaussée*, leaving two guns upon it. Between eleven and twelve a.m. the

A MOUNTED ROCKET TROOPER

UNIFORM OF THE ROYAL HORSE ARTILLERY

enemy commence the attack with a tremendous cannonade, under cover of which they advance their columns, directing them upon the heights on each side of the *chaussée*, and upon a brow and village upon the right of our position. Their attacks are repeated and repeated until their last effort is made, between seven and eight p.m., which being defeated and the Prussians having approached their right and rear, the army are thrown into utter confusion, and a complete rout ensues, leaving the whole of their artillery on the field of battle.

My troop halts for the night with the Guards near Belle Alliance. I return to headquarters with Wood and Dickson to enquire about my wounded friends.

June 19th.—March to Nivelle. Headquarters, Brussels.

June 20th.—To Villers St. Gislin. Headquarters, Nivelle.

June 21st.—Malplaquet. Headquarters, Bavay.

June 22nd.—Bavay.

June 24th.—Englefontaine. King Louis XVIII. passed on his way to the duke's headquarters at Le Cateau.

June 25th.—Marets.

June 26th.—Near Bellinglieu.

June 27th.—Ham.

June 28th.—Near Roye.

June 29th.—Gournay.

June 30th.—Pont St. Maxence.

July 1st.—Louvres.

July 2nd.—Garges.

The letters which follow are from Colonel Sir Augustus Frazer, commanding the Horse Artillery of the army, and relate to the equipment of Sir Hew Ross's battery for the Waterloo campaign.

The Horse Artillery had been equipped in the Peninsula with light 6-prs. and 12-pr. howitzers: for the new campaign it was determined—as will be seen from these letters—that they should be equipped with 9-prs. and 24-pr. howitzers. One battery, Colonel Bull's, was equipped with 24-pr. howitzers only.

BRITISH 6-PR GUN

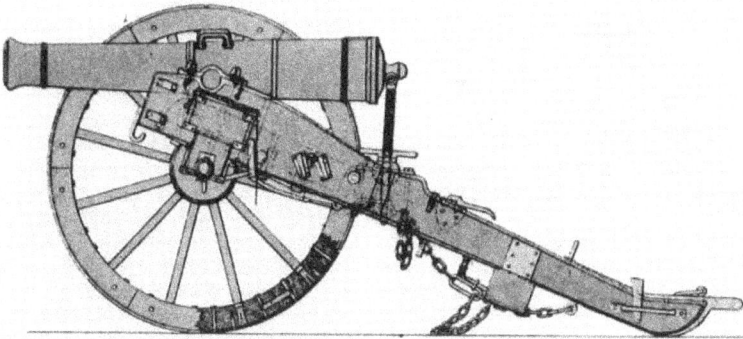

BRITISH 9-PR GUN

Ostend,

April 25, 1815.

My dear Ross,

I hear with great pleasure that you are coming to join us; we want all hands to assist in the strength, and shall be most glad to see you.

Gardiner has, I believe, apprised you that our troops are reforming on the Peninsular system; not satisfied with the advantages of which, we are compromising the matter by adding the inconveniences in the shape of the heavy 6-prs. those duck guns which you had ingenuity enough to avoid receiving. Bring out your own personal equipment, just as before—pack-saddle, &c, &c.; but this is a luxurious country compared with Spain. I have returned from head-quarters to assist in the arrangement and distribution of the mass of ordnance and stores arrived and arriving here, and Stace being come from England has already done wonders, so that I trust to be permitted to return to my more legitimate employment in the charge of the Horse Artillery.

Yesterday I selected drivers and horses (or rather told off, there being no surplus of either after the appropriation) from the Driver Corps for the four British and two German troops of Horse Artillery. The horses are generally good, the men may be made so, and I trust both will be transferred at once to the Horse Artillery. Till that is done we have the old story of two families, and nominal returns and open accounts with every troop in the service.

There is nothing new. We are up late and early, work hard, and are in consequence in good health. Macdonald and Mercer have moved from Ghent to Thermonde, whither Gardiner, who marched two days ago, is following them. This movement was merely to leave Ghent a little more open. Thermonde is the Dendermond, celebrated for the siege of my Uncle Toby. . . .

Adieu. Nothing new. Remember me to my friends of "A" Troop. Bring with you your 200 animals—that is if you can. There can be no doubt about the establishment, nor that all minor considerations must give way to making complete those troops which are to be employed here. Why won't they send out Norman Ramsay? If Dickson is to come, let him be sent openly. He is a noble fellow, and fit for anything; but don't let my old troop be without Ramsay.

I am,

Yours sincerely,

Aug. S. Frazer.

An Officer, Private & Driver of the Royal Wagon Train

The next letter notifies the equipment decided upon for Sir Hew Ross's battery:—

Brussels,
May 24, 1815.

My dear Ross,

You know our late changes of ordnance; another is about to take place in our troops. I am to see my Lord Uxbridge on the subject early tomorrow morning at Ninove, and I now write, as I may not be able tomorrow. I shall not send my letter unless the expected arrangement for your troop be ordered. If it should, my writing today may be useful.

Your troop will consist of five 9-prs. and one heavy 5½ howitzer, seven 9-pr. ammunition wagons and two heavy 5½ howitzer wagons, a spare 9-pr. gun-carriage with wheels, a forge wagon, store wagon, and curricle cart. Whatever part of this equipment you can receive at Ostend will be so much the better. You can exchange there the 6-prs. you may have brought from England. Whatever cannot be exchanged at Ostend, we must exchange when and where we can.

According to this arrangement your ammunition will be:—

9-pr. gun .... 32 $\Big\}$ 116.
Wagon 84
One-fifth of two reserve wagons ...... $\frac{192}{5}$ = $\frac{44}{155}$ rounds for each 9-pr.

Heavy 5½ howitzer :—

Limbers.. 24
Wagon 60
Reserve do. 60
_____
144 rounds for howitzer.

It is my intention that you shall have no men on limbers of your guns, but that your mounted detachment shall be of ten men each. If my letters to this effect reached England before you were equipped, provision will have been made for this, both as to your number of gunners and also of their appointments. Should this not be the case, we must manage as well as we can till the requested reinforcement shall arrive.

I hope that you have at least been completed at home to the 197 animals of which troops now consist. This establishment will, I hope, very soon receive an addition of horses, as I hope there will also be an addition to that of the men. Perhaps you may bring with you the additional mounted men for all the troops which I have requested.

Adieu. We have reviews almost daily; two days ago, of the Brunswickers (7000) near Vilvorde, today of the heavy cavalry, tomorrow of the hussars, and on Monday of all the cavalry and the Horse Artillery. I would my old friends of "A" were there.

Yours sincerely,

Aug. S. Frazer.

Many thanks for the writing case. I am running more, too, in your debt, for a saddle, &c, which I find you are bringing.

Remember me to Parker, Hardinge, &c.

P.S.—May 25th.—Stace has written to Mr. Walker, Commissary at Ostend, to give you twelve saddles and bridles for the twelve additional mounted men for your detachments, which will be of ten mounted men each. Choose the very best horses you can, so as to attach eight to each carriage and have four spare ones. This moment (2 p.m.) from Ninove—-where Lord Uxbridge has arranged the troops as I supposed—Bell, Smith, and Whinyates march immediately to the neighbourhood of Grammont. More tomorrow. Excuse haste. Adye will, I am sure, give you every aid.

Aug. S. Frazer.

★★★★★★

Brussels,
May 27, 1815.

My dear Ross,

My letter of the 25th inst., directed to you at Ostend, will have apprised you that your troop is to have five 9-prs., one heavy 5½ howitzer, seven 9-pr. wagons, and two howitzer *ditto*. Your establishment of drivers will be 85, and your total number of animals will be 220.

I trust the ordnance required for the exchange will be provided at Ostend on your arrival, and I have written to Adye to supply you with the drivers and horses necessary to complete you to the proposed establishment, and I have begged him to give you the best, which no doubt he will do. Whatever further you may wish to have exchanged I have no doubt Adye will exchange for you, as he is fully convinced of the necessity that the Horse Artillery should be well equipped.

I have received yours of the 17th from Woolwich. It is too bad that the energy which all of us shew in getting our troops ready should not be met by equal energy on the part of those who have it in their power to assist us. I continue to write strongly, and in my last letter urged so forcibly the necessity of sending hither instantly sixty mounted men that I think it can hardly be parried.

Adieu. I write not in my best case. But we had a ball last night at

111

the Duke's, and the ladies were fair and the champagne bright, *et c'est pourquoi*. I feel good for nothing. Moreover, his lordship of Uxbridge is to shew the cavalry and Horse Artillery to the duke on Monday, and we are all preparation. Smith and Whinyates marched yesterday, and Bell marches tomorrow, and all for this review, which will be at Schandelbeke, near Grammont.

Yours sincerely,

Aug. S. Frazer.

Do they talk of Wilmot's coming? If not, I wish they would break his troop up and send it and Bean's here to complete us.

★★★★★★

Brussels,
June 1, 1815.

My dear Ross,

My letter of the 27th *ultimo* will have acquainted you that your troop is to have five 9-prs. and one heavy 5½ howitzer. Bell will by this post send you the proposed establishment of drivers and horses.

By Saunders' letter to me of the 23rd May, you will bring 190 horses and 73 drivers from England. You will accordingly want 12 drivers and 30 horses.

You will also require that your spare gun-carriage should be a 9-pr. one; and you will want, moreover, I presume, three—and probably five—9-pr. ammunition wagons, and one heavy 5½ howitzer wagon. Further, you will require the necessary harness. You are aware, I believe, that all your detachments are to consist of ten mounted men, each told off as per list below.

9, 2, 7, 10, 11, } without men
12, 3, 8, 13, 1, } on limbers.
Or,
9, 2, 14, 10, 11, } with 7 or 8
12, 3, 15, 13, 1, } on limbers.

With respect to equipment, the general *outline* should be on the Peninsular system; but lots of everything is required in this abundant country. The general order relative to tents will explain this point. Your troop will not in the first instance be applied to cavalry, but with the two German ones, and that coming from England (all of which four troops are to be similarly armed with five 9-prs. and one howitzer), will remain disposable.

As I hope, and Saunders assures me that you will bring with you thirty-six saddles and bridles for the general service of the troops here, you are fairly entitled to take whatever number you may require for your own troop, to complete to the ten required for each of the six detachments; only bring the remainder with you to Ghent, and let me know what that number is, and what you have taken, that I may arrange their distribution. At present, having seized on the saddles of all the clerks and conductors of stores, I have thirty saddles in hand, but they are without pads, which to avoid expense I shall not put to them until I hear from you.

I will say when the wants mentioned in the first part of my letter shall be supplied, when Bell—whom I have sent to Sir John May—shall have returned.

You will believe that I have spared no pains to get the proper establishment for the troops. I have rated this in the 9-pr. troops at 100 gunners and additional artificers, and I trust to carry the point, though I have not time now to explain it.

Get your troop to Ghent as soon as you can, that I may have the pleasure of coming to see one in which Wood and myself recollect to have passed some of the happiest days of our lives.

Pray bring with you, to oblige me, a small box and paper parcel, belonging to Colonel Cameron, 92nd Regiment, which are at Ostend with Paymaster Rowen, 13th Veteran Battalion. You must have —— for the appointments, and the things will not inconvenience you in addition.

P.S.—Thirty horses are ordered to be selected for you at Ghent.

The twelve drivers will be given to you at Ostend from those hourly expected. The harness you may get at Ostend; the spare 9-pr. gun-carriage you may get at Ghent.

Your ordnance you will get at Ghent—that is when it shall be received there from England, whence it has not yet been received.

Remember me to all friends. Tell Hardinge I saw his brother at the Schandelbeke review two days ago, when he was well, and, like everyone, in the highest spirits. 5600 such salvoes, and 36 such guns!

Yours sincerely,

Aug. S. Frazer.

★★★★★★

Headquarters, Brussels,
June 4, 1815.

My dear Ross,

I have yours of the 2nd June, from Saas. I had not time yesterday

113

to write more than a general assurance that all your wants shall be supplied; let me today repeat the assurance. You will reach Ghent on Monday, the 5th inst. I am very desirous of inspecting the troop as soon as possible, with the view of losing no time in making all necessary demands. I will therefore be at Ghent on Tuesday, the 8th inst. I will be there by four p.m., and will either inspect the troop then or at seven on Wednesday morning, as you may arrange with reference to your own convenience.

I must return to Brussels on the 7th. Perhaps you will come with me, and leave your name at the duke's. I have a bed and stable for you. I shall drive over in a gig with Maxwell, and we will dine with you on Tuesday.

Pray tell Newland that if the sixty remount horses have not marched for the several troops, I will see them with your troop, which I presume by that time the thirty horses and six drivers ordered you, will have joined.

May sends today an order for six more drivers to join you, which I think will complete you.

You have done quite right about wagons; you are doomed to have 9-prs. *Sans remède,* and I am an advocate for them, as the duke is so too. *Gare à qui* shall speak to their disadvantage.

Stace is at Antwerp, so is Pickering the paymaster, Butcher not being so till 1st July. But I'll get money for you and bring it with me; it is indispensable that you should have some forthwith.

Write by return of post, should there be any use in your doing so, if you have any difficulty in completing your ordnance, carriage, harness, and appointments at Ghent; but I both hope and believe there will be none.

Ward has gone to the commissary-general to secure your commissary, who shall join without delay.

You must lose Hardinge, who by the duke's directions, communicated to him by Lord Fitzroy, is 'to join his brother at Namur and act as his secretary.'

Now it may be of some importance to you to have a good successor, therefore let me know who I shall apply for from home, and write to the same tenor yourself; only send me word tomorrow, that I may not lose the mail, which is made up here by ten a.m. on Tuesdays and Fridays. Morrison or Younghusband, or whoever is senior, will doubtless accommodate you with an orderly, should it be inconvenient to send one of your own after the march.

I saw my Lord Uxbridge at a ball at Sir Charles Stuart's last night. His lordship was particularly anxious to get the three small boxes you have brought for Lady Uxbridge, and I told his lordship I had begged you to send them as soon as possible, promising to forward them instantly from here by an orderly. If they are transportable, pray send them by the earliest mode which presents itself. A wagon might readily be pressed. In this case my parcels might come; otherwise I am in no violent hurry.

Lord Uxbridge is anxious to have your troop, but the duke has otherwise arranged.

The Prussian review is put off. I wrote to Hardinge to mention his appointment at Namur.

Pray mount me when I come to inspect you, to save stud. I only send a relay to Alost. Make up your mind to return with me, and when you shall have had a peep at the fair Bruxillians, Parker may take half an one, which is as much as married men can be allowed.

Yours sincerely,

Aug. S. Frazer.

I have papers and letters for Jenkinson a yard high, but know not where my lord is, though doubtless in great force somewhere.

I do not yet make out whether you have brought any saddles and bridles for other troops; a late letter from Woolwich led me to suppose thirty-six of each would accompany your troop.

P.S.—Pray let Newland know that "E" Troop has marched to Jernath this morning, and Whinyates to Parnell. Gardiner does not mention where Jernath is, but I presume but a little way from Parnell. Both places are near Ninove, where cavalry headquarters are.

★★★★★★

Brussels,
June 6, 1815, 10 a.m.

My dear Ross,

I have just received yours of the 2nd, which has by some accident been delayed.

I make out from it that some horse appointments were in Mr Walker's store at Ostend, and that they will, or rather, correctly speaking, have been forwarded to Ghent. I trust they are the identical thirty-six saddles and bridles expected by me to have been sent with your troop from Woolwich.

I hear, too, from Mr. Benton, commissary here, that he had an account from Mr. Walker of six (I believe) vats for the Horse Artillery, marked for the several troops, but of the contents of which he has no invoice or knowledge. I conclude from all this that the vats contain the appointments expected, and under that persuasion have requested Mr. Benton to desire Mr. Currie to send early tomorrow morning by a wagon hither all the vats in question, after you shall have taken what may be requisite to complete your troop.

I presume the thirty-six saddles, &c. to have been demanded on the original supposition that all the troops would have three heavy pieces; but as it has since been arranged that "E" and "F" have only one heavy piece (the howitzer), it is clear that the saddles are applicable to other troops. Accordingly, by whatever number you may be short of seventy saddles and bridles (of which number I wish your troop and the other 9-pr. ones to consist), pray take; only send off as early as possible to-morrow the remainder to Brussels, sending someone with the wagon or wagons; and pray send Bell and Maxwell a memorandum on the subject, that no time may be lost in desiring the troops in this neighbourhood to send hither for their proportion of the saddles.

Pray send the boxes for Lord Uxbridge, my saddle, and also the box (size and contents unknown) said to have reached Ghent for the Rocket Troop.

I hope Wood and Percy Drummond will accompany Maxwell and myself to Ghent tomorrow. On arriving—which we shall do at or about four p.m.—pray have someone at the Brussels Gate to say where you are to be found and what your arrangements are.

Aug. S. Frazer.

P.S.—Since writing the above, Mr. Benton has produced a memorandum from Mr. Walker, by which it would seem that the vats may contain clothing and not saddles.

Pray break them open; if saddles, arrange for yourself, and send forward what you do not want, as above mentioned.

If clothing or anything else, pray let me have a memorandum on seeing you at dinner.

Nothing very new today.

Ever yours sincerely,

Aug. S. Frazer.

The following copy of a reply given in 1835 to an enquiry from Captain Siborne, the constructor of the Waterloo model at the United Service Institution, contains the only reference to the position of the

Chestnut Troop at Waterloo, or to the part which it took in the action, to be found in Sir Hew Ross's correspondence:—

To Captain Siborne

Carlisle,
January 27, 1835.

Sir,

I am sorry to have detained the enclosed plan of the field of Waterloo so long. I did so in the expectation that I should be able to give satisfactory answers to the several questions contained in your letter respecting the formations and movements of the enemy that came under my immediate observation in the course of that battle, but I regret to say I find it quite impossible to do so in a manner to satisfy myself; as at this distant period, and after much consideration, I feel that I cannot separate what I may fairly charge to my memory from the impressions left on it by what I have since heard and read of that eventful day; added to which I have never been on the ground since the day of the action. Under these circumstances, I cannot reconcile myself to giving an opinion upon questions of such importance without being quite sure that I am accurate.

With respect to my own troop, it was posted at the commencement of the day—two guns on the road at the quarry, and four on the heights to its right, where it was exposed to a destructive fire, by which three guns were disabled; and when the enemy's cavalry forced that part of the position, several men were cut down before they could take shelter behind the infantry. After the enemy got possession of La Haye Sainte it was no longer possible to remain in our first position, and the troop was ordered to take ground to its right. At the moment the French Imperial Guards reached the crest of the position, in their last attack, it occupied, as near as I can now judge, the situation I have marked upon the plan, though I cannot speak positively as to the precise spot; and on the repulse of the enemy, the three guns then moveable joined in the pursuit to the heights beyond La Belle Alliance.

I have the honour to be,
&c., &c., &c.,

H. D. Ross .

Sir Hew Ross's active service closed with the peace which followed the Battle of Waterloo. He was then, though only a regimental captain of the Royal Artillery, a lieut.-colonel in the army and a Knight Commander of the Bath; and the position in the estimation

BATTLE OF
WATERLOO
18th June 1815
CRISIS OF THE BATTLE

Allies ▭ French
Cavalry ▭ Infantry ▦ Artillery

SCALE OF 1 ENGLISH MILE

of the army at large to which he and his brother officers of the same rank had raised their battery commands is well shown by the following letter, addressed to him as commanding officer of his battery by the Duke of York, which Sir Hew Ross had preserved with his private papers. The letter is also of interest as notifying the first grant of a general medal in the British Army:—

Horse Guards,
March 23, 1816.

Sir,

The prince regent having been graciously pleased, in the name and on the behalf of His Majesty, to command that a medal should be struck for the officers and men who fought at the Battle of Waterloo, I have the satisfaction to transmit to you the medals for the officers and men of the troop of Royal Horse Artillery under your command; and I am to desire that you will pay the strictest attention to the distribution of these honourable badges of distinction according to the names mentioned in the accompanying list; and as several of the officers may have been promoted, removed, or placed on half-pay, and many of the non-commissioned officers and private soldiers may have been transferred, discharged, or have died, I am further to desire that in all such cases you will return the medals to my office, with such information in regard to the places of abode of the individuals—especially the officers—as you may have it in your power to give.

The medal is to be worn on the breast, or to the button-hole of the uniform, suspended by the ribbon which is in the box; and it must be distributed in the proportion of a quarter of a yard to each medal.

I am, Sir,

Yours,

Frederick,
Commander-in-Chief.

Lieut.-Colonel Sir H. D. Ross, K.C.B.,
Royal Horse Artillery,
Woolwich.

In a speech on the Ordnance Estimates in 1845, the late General Sir Howard Douglas, Bart., made the following reference to the services of the Horse Artillery in general, and of Sir Hew Ross's battery in particular, and it will be gratifying to artillery officers to read the terms in which these were referred to by that officer, and by an even better and more unbiassed judge, the late General Sir George Murray,

119

then Master-General of the Ordnance:—

Sir H. Douglas entreated the committee not to be led away by the hon. member's regard for pecuniary economy to interfere with this splendid and efficient corps—the Horse Artillery. . . He (Sir H. Douglas) would not attempt to take up the time of the committee to trace this. For this, it would be necessary to go back to the time of Frederick the Great, who introduced Horse Artillery in that war in which, by celerity of movement, he defeated, with the same army, enemies on every frontier of his states. He might show the prodigious advantages reaped in all the armies of Europe from the adoption of this arm—the important uses made of it by Dumourier, Pichegru, and Napoleon; and in our own service, the brilliant services of that corps in the Peninsular war. He (Sir H. Douglas) would not attempt to specify the many brilliant proofs exhibited in that war of the peculiar advantages of that description of artillery to which the hon. member's observations relate, but, with the permission of the committee, would refer only to the Battle of the Nivelle, on the 10th of November, 1813.

Clauzel was strongly posted on a ridge, having the village of Sarre in front, covered by two formidable redoubts—San Barbe and Grenada. He thought the country in front was so difficult and impracticable for artillery, that he was astonished when eighteen British guns opened upon those redoubts at daylight in the morning. Under the powerful effect of a shower of shot poured upon San Barbe, the infantry of the 4th Division stormed and carried that redoubt. Ross (the present Sir Hew) then galloped—he (Sir H. Douglas) begged the committee to mark the term—galloped to a rising ground in rear of the other redoubt, Grenada, drove the enemy from it, when the British infantry carried it and the village of Sarre, and advanced to the attack of Clauzel's main position.

Part of it was carried, but Clauzel stood firm, covered by another redoubt and a powerful battery. These were speedily silenced by Ross's troop of Horse Artillery, the only battery that had been able to surmount the difficulties of the ground after passing Sarre. The British infantry then carried the redoubt, drove Clauzel from his position, forced the French to retire, and the rout was complete. Sir, that operation was worth all the money the Horse Artillery ever cost the country.

The following day Sir Howard Douglas wrote as follows:—

Green Street,
Saturday.

My dear Ross,

I spoke out last night in defence and eulogy of the Horse Artillery, and the inadequacy of the numbers of the corps for all the demands upon it. . . .

I consign to you Murray's letter, which does you and the corps so much honour.

Ever affectionately yours,

Howard Douglas.

(Enclosure.)

General Sir George Murray, G.C.B., to General Sir Howard Douglas.

6, Belgrave Square,
May 19, 1845.

My dear Sir Howard,

The action to which I alluded when you were here on Sunday was that which is detailed in the Duke of Wellington's despatch, dated at St. Pé, on the 13th November, 1813.

The circumstance of the action to which I particularly adverted was the carrying of two field works which the French had constructed in front of the village of Sarre, and considerably in advance of the centre of the general line of their fortified position. The possession of these field works was an indispensable prelude to the attack of the main position on the commanding heights above Sarre. To carry them, however, without the aid of a powerful and well-served artillery, would have proved both a tedious and a costly operation; but the roads leading towards them, over steep mountains and over rocky and difficult ravines, were almost totally impracticable for any description of wheel carriage.

Over these roads, however, the British Horse Artillery forced their way in spite of every obstacle, aided by the superior quality of all its equipments, the excellence of its horses, and the skill and energy of every officer and soldier of the corps; and the enemy's troops, notwithstanding their gallantry, were effectually dislodged from their works, almost before they could have recovered from their astonishment at seeing three brigades of artillery open against them, which had arrived by mountain passes which seemed sufficient of themselves to secure them from so sudden and so efficient an attack by that arm.

Nor was the advantage confined to the dislodgement of the enemy from the field works in front of Sarre; for the promptitude with which that was effected contributed in the most material manner to the complete success which immediately followed in the attack of the enemy's main position in the commanding and fortified heights behind, which was so rapid that one entire French battalion had not time to extricate itself from the redoubt which it occupied before it was compelled to capitulate.

Such events clearly demonstrate that the truest economy in war is to have in every branch of the service the best and most efficient means for making war which the skill and the wealth of the country is able to produce.

> Believe me always,
> My dear Sir Howard,
> Very faithfully yours,
>
> G. Murray.
> Lieut.-General

Sir Howard Douglas, Bart.,
G.C.B.

Sir Hew Ross remained with the Army of Occupation till December, 1815, when he returned to England. In the following year he married Elizabeth Margaret, daughter of Richard Graham, Esq., of Stonehouse, near Carlisle. He continued to serve with the Chestnut Troop, first at Lewes, and then in Ireland, at Dublin, and Athlone, till promoted to a Regimental Lieut.-Colonelcy, in July, 1825.

In 1823 he received the following letter from Lord Fitzroy Somerset, offering him the Brigade-Majorship of the Royal Artillery in Ireland:—

> Ordnance Office,
> June 27, 1823.

My dear Ross,

As the situation of Brigade-Major in Ireland will become vacant on the promotion of Colonel Bull, which will probably take place in less than a fortnight, I am desired by the master-general to inform you that he shall be happy to nominate you to that appointment, if it should be agreeable to you.

The duke is aware that you have already been nine years in Ireland, and that perhaps it may not suit you to return to that country; but he is anxious to seize this opportunity of shewing his regard for your services, and of evincing his desire of serving you when it may be in his power.

Yours faithfully,

(Signed) Fitzroy Somerset.

Writing to one of his sisters, July 15th, 1823, he refers as follows to his answer:—

Since my return from London I have had a tempting offer to return to Ireland, on the Staff, as brigade-major to the artillery. It was made in a very kind manner by the Duke of Welling-ton, but on consideration of Elizabeth's health and that of her mother, with other circumstances, I thought it best to decline it. Had my troop continued there, and I had to join, it would have been a most eligible situation, giving a good house in Dublin, and near £200 a-year.

The following year, upon hearing a report of expected promo-tions, he wrote to Lord Fitzroy Somerset to mention his wish to be re-appointed to the Horse Artillery:—

Stonehouse, Brampton, Cumberland,
June 24, 1824.

My dear Lord,

Some of my friends write me word that a report is prevalent with them that the general officers of the corps are about to be removed from their regimental commissions; and as in the event of such an arrangement I should be deprived of my troop, without waiting to calculate the chances for or against the probability of the rumour, I have at once resolved to solicit your lordship's interposition in my fa-vour, by bringing my name (if you think it proper) under the master-general's notice as a candidate (should my promotion take place) for a continuance in the service of the Horse Artillery.

As any pretension I have to His Grace's favour is already known to your lordship, I feel it only necessary, as due to myself, to express the grateful sense I have of your kindness to me on former occasions, and to request you will in this instance employ your friendly offices for me in the manner you may think most respectful on my part to the Duke of Wellington, and most likely to promote the object of this application.

To this, Lord Fitzroy Somerset sent the following answer :—

Ordnance Office,
June 28, 1821.

My dear Colonel,

I have received your letter of the 24th instant. There is not now any question of the removal of the general officers of the artillery from their regimental commissions, but even if that measure were resolved upon, and the promotion consequent upon it were to take place, I would strongly advise you to make no application to the master-general for the appointment in the Horse Artillery which Colonel Bull would vacate. Your services are so well known to His Grace, and he has always evinced so favourable a disposition towards you, that in my opinion it would be judicious in you to leave your interests entirely in his hands, without attempting to press your claims upon his attention.

Yours faithfully,

(Signed)   Fitzroy Somerset.

Sir Hew Ross's promotion to a regimental lieut.-colonelcy occurred on the 29th July, 1825, and he was then re-appointed at once to the Horse Artillery. The following letter to his sisters shows that he had acted on Lord Fitzroy Somerset's advice, and was specially gratified by the receipt of his appointment through the Duke of Wellington's own appreciation of his services:—

My dear sisters, rejoice with me; I am a lieut.-colonel of Horse Artillery! I yesterday received a note from Lord Fitzroy Somerset to tell me of my promotion to a lieut.-colonelcy in the regiment, and that the Duke of Wellington had nominated me to the Horse Artillery. It is a great event for me in every point of view, and at this moment I ought to be more than ever thankful to a kind Providence that by this step has removed from me the dread of being separated from my family. By it my service in times of peace will be confined to England and Ireland, which, looking to my increasing family, is a most important advantage, and has relieved my mind from a weight of care.

Had I not been named by the duke to the service of the Horse Artillery, the notification of my promotion might have brought me also an order to embark for a colony in the West Indies, or elsewhere. The manner in which it has been done is particularly gratifying; for knowing that His Grace does not like to be plagued with applications, I made none, either personally or through my friends. I have therefore solely to thank him, and feel grateful for his recollection of my past services. I have no idea where I may be stationed, perhaps in Sussex, but nothing can now come amiss to me.

A letter of the 25th August, 1825, from Sir John Macleod, then Deputy-Adjutant-General of Artillery, explains the reason of his wish for the command of the artillery in Sussex not being acceded to:—

My dear Ross,

In regard to the wish you express about Sussex, I am sorry to have to say that there is an obstacle, and that it is one which you will be inclined to feel about as I do. I cannot, however, but hope the northern district, being so immediately in your neighbourhood, and the duty such as will enable you to have constant intercourse with home, that the change will not appear to you in the shape of a great disappointment.

You know Sir John May has been in extreme ill-health, and although now improved into a convalescent, yet the sea and the situation have been considered by his medical advisers as the best means of restoring him. It makes no difference as to future movements, they being alike detachments from the headquarters...... Let me hear from you. Nothing will be proceeded in till we hear from or see our duke, and you need not disturb yourself until you hear from me.

Believe me,
My dear Ross,
Sincerely yours,
J. Macleod.

On the 17th September, 1825, Sir John Macleod writes again:—

The order retaining all the colonels in their several commands has indeed overset all our projects and arrangements, and I fear leaves me little to say than that we remain as we were before. You will therefore continue upon leave of absence.

Sir Hew Ross was appointed soon after this date to the command of the Royal Artillery in the northern district, then commanded by General Sir John Byng, afterwards Lord Strafford. Upon applying to Sir John Byng for instructions where he was to make his headquarters, informing him that he had a house near Carlisle at which, if it met his approval, he should be glad to reside, Sir John Byng stated that he should be glad to have an officer of Sir Hew Ross's standing in that portion of the district, and that he would give him a delegated command of the troops in its four northern counties. Sir Hew Ross continued to hold this command, under Sir John Byng and his successors, till his appointment to be Deputy-Adjutant-General of Artillery, in 1841. The manufacturing districts were more or less disturbed during the greater part of this period, and a few extracts are given from the letters he received and wrote while in the northern district which shew the critical state of the country and the nature of his duties.

To his sister

Manchester,
May 15, 1826.

As you may be curious to know how we are going on, I find great pleasure in telling you that here and in the surrounding country everything continues perfectly tranquil. Distress, I am sorry to say, has not disappeared, but it has been greatly mitigated, and I do not apprehend any renewal of riot. The prospect of trade is partially improved, and I hope ere long we shall see it become general; and when the poor can find employment, the disposition to disturb the peace of the country will disappear with the cause that produced it.

To the same

Stonehouse,
June 7, 1826.

You will be sorry to hear that there was an election riot yesterday at Carlisle, in which some lives were lost. All has since been quiet, and I hope the peace will not again be disturbed.

From the Mayor of Carlisle:—

In consequence of the disposition of the populace to riot, I request that the military under your command may not leave Carlisle. Dated this 6th June, 1826.
(Signed) ———
Mayor.

This application was minuted at the back as follows:—

6th June, 1826.

From the Mayor of Carlisle. His request not complied with. The cavalry sent to villages distant from the city more than two miles.
(Signed) H. D. Ross.

A similar application on the 10th June, 1826, met with the same fate:—

Sir,

In consequence of the riots which took place here yesterday, and the obstructions given by the mob to the voters coming to the poll, I request, with the advice of Mr. ——, my assessor, that you will assemble the troops under your orders at the town hall.

(Signed) ————

Mayor.

To the Officer Commanding at Carlisle.

Docket.—10th June, 1826. From the Mayor of Carlisle. His request not complied with. The infantry remain in the Castle Barracks. The cavalry ordered to assemble in Botcherby Lane, about a mile from the city, and to wait there for orders.

(Signed) H. D. R.

Received by Sir Hew about 10 a.m. on Saturday. Delivered by Captain Whale, 5th Dragoon Guards.

The following letter to Sir John Byng contains a report on the riots of the 6th June, and the causes of the troops being so frequently called upon by the civil power:—

Carlisle,
June 14, 1826.

Dear Sir,

I had the honour to receive your letter of the 9th instant on Sunday, and I am this morning favoured with one from Colonel Riddell, in which he informs me that you wish to know my private opinion of the lamentable affair that took place here on the 6th instant.

In such cases it is always a difficult matter to get at the truth, and more especially when party feeling naturally gives rise to exaggeration; but from the best information I have been able to procure, I am decidedly of opinion that at the time the aid of the troops was called for, there was no other means of obtaining the release of the candidate (Sir Philip Musgrave), and afterwards of the mayor—the total absence of conduct, or proper organisation of the civil power, having placed them completely at the mercy of the mob.

And I am also fully satisfied that when the infantry did arrive at the scene of riot, it was not only necessary to use force to rescue them, but that they (the infantry) were compelled to do so in their own defence; Captain Gardiner (the senior officer) being knocked down, and several officers and men severely braised by large stones, before the magistrate called upon them to fire.

How far Captain Gardiner may have used a proper discretion in allowing himself to be influenced by the desire of the magistrate to fire, rather than use the bayonet, I am not prepared to say; for although, had it been my case, I should have preferred the latter, I think it fair to remark that he had to deal with young soldiers, and might not think it prudent to bring them, in a state of irritation, in contact with the mob.

With respect to the cavalry not having been employed in preference to clear the streets, although I understand they turned out with the greatest alacrity (being in billets), the infantry were brought from the castle in a much shorter time than they could assemble. It is unfortunate that they were not waited for; but the apprehended danger to Sir P. Musgrave and the mayor appear to have prompted an immediate attempt for their release.

From the best information I can collect, I have no reason to believe that there is any truth in the report that individuals of the 55th Regiment fired wantonly at private houses; that they may have fired indiscreetly is but too probable, for many of them are mere recruits, and it is most likely they never took aim at all.

I enclose Lieut. Luard's report to me. He was present during the whole affair, and I believe it to be an accurate statement, and I have great pleasure in adding that I have received the most gratifying accounts of his conduct. He assures me that in the onset of the riot, he would have been bound, with a few resolute followers, to have rescued Sir P. Musgrave, and to have seized the ringleaders; but in this city there are, I believe, only two constables, and if there were any *special* ones, they did not act.

As this state of things must at every election, as well as on occasions of any other disturbances, however trifling, subject the military force to be called in aid of the civil power, I am anxious that you should be aware of it; and I also beg leave to trouble you with copies of the notes that passed between the mayor and myself on Saturday, the 10th inst., to show you how completely he intended to place himself under the protection of the troops. Upon receiving the first, being very unwilling to bring the 55th Regiment again in contact with the populace, and at the opening of the poll seeing no riot, I sent Captain Wheeler to know if he required the infantry before the arrival of the dragoons.

Fortunately, he dispensed with the actual appearance of either, but the dragoons being seen on the outskirts of the town, gave rise to a violent speech by Mr. W. Brougham on the hustings, when the mob assailed the mayor, and compelled him to write the last note. He was immediately afterwards taken so ill that he was conveyed from the hustings, and on Monday Mr. Holt acted in his place, and closed the election.

On Sunday, two gentlemen (Sir J. Gilpin and Mr. Nanson) called upon me with a message from the mayor, to say he intended to call upon me to assemble a force at the town hall on the following morning, before the poll should be opened. I again expressed my opinion that the troops ought not to be called out, except in case of actual riot, and in answer was told he had the best legal advice, and knew his responsibility.

The mayor did not act on Monday, and the presence of the troops was not required.

I am sorry I have carried my story to such a length, but I am anxious to put you in possession of the whole of the case, and I hope I shall appear to you to have acted with sufficient caution in only bringing the dragoons within a mile of the town on Saturday, and requiring a further demand before I allowed them to enter it.

I have the honour to be,

&c, &c, &c,

H. D. Ross.
Lieut.-General

Sir John Byng, K.C.B.,
&c, &c, &c.

An official approval of the conduct of the troops on this occasion is contained in the following letter from the Home Office:—

My dear Sir,

Mr. Peel desires me to say that he is much pleased at the result of the enquiry into the affair at Carlisle, which has completely removed the erroneous impression he was under that the troops had acted at least injudiciously.

At the same time, the circumstances of this ease strengthen his belief that in a great majority of instances it would be better for the military to charge than to fire.

Yours truly,

(Signed)

H. Hobhouse.

To Lieut.-General
Sir John Byng, K.C.B.,
&c., &c., &c.

★★★★★★

After further experience of the use of small bodies of troops in riots, it was decided that when called upon to act they were at once to do so effectually, as the most humane as well as most effective course.

★★★★★★

Sir W. Clinton's expedition to Portugal, at the commencement of 1827, called for the equipment of a small force of field artillery, which was conducted on a most economical scale. The following extracts from letters received by Sir Hew Ross from his friends at Woolwich, show the feelings with which they regarded inefficient establishments, and have interest as artillery records:—

From Colonel Bull, Commanding Royal Horse Artillery at Woolwich.

December 22, 1826

Burgoyne, one captain, and one subaltern of the Engineers, are gone, and a company of the Staff Corps. Webber Smith sailed from the arsenal yesterday afternoon at two o'clock, with his three brigades of four guns each, and one brigade of ball cartridge carts, with Lieut. Bridges as adjutant, and Lieut. Wightman, of the Invalids, as quartermaster (Smith's old sergt.-major). The companies were Major Wilgress's, Taylor's, Bridges', and Wylde's (the latter changed with Bob Douglas). O'Connor went out as veterinary surgeon; Verling and Seaton of our medical department.

The guns were 9-prs. and 24-pr. howitzers. They had each six horses, and the wagons each four horses. They had the old forge, store wagon and spare gun and wheel carriage to each brigade. The ball cartridge carts are, it is thought, and may prove, an improvement. They are, in fact, wagons, the body carrying 12,000 and the limbers 8000 rounds, making 20,000, all packed in small flat boxes, and the flints in a separate box lashed on the top of the perch, where the spare wheel rode on the store wagon. These carts are the old 6-pr. wagon and wheels.

When I have said thus much, you have the total of W. Smith's command, as you can easily give him a fair proportion of spare and requisite stores. Of the horses, all young, and insufficient in number if they have marches to perform, with few spare, and drivers who weigh, some about 18st. themselves, who can neither ride, drive, or take care of a horse, you may think with me that Smith has an arduous task, and so I believe he thinks; but as any of the dear old H.A. leaven would do, he will make the best of it, and I have no doubt will do all that man could do. But these things are not fair, after all the experience we have had.

From the same.

February 9, 1827.

Since my last, the death of his late Royal Highness the commander-in-chief has produced changes which the public prints will have informed, you of. Things still look very gloomy in the military circles, and few talk of the change. I have reason to think that no material change will take place in the Ordnance at present; but the expected resignation of Sir Herbert Taylor may remove Lord Fitzroy from the Ordnance Office, and perhaps, if business accumulates in the various departments, we may have a lieut.-general resident. But my principal motive for writing at this moment in the haste I do, is to tell you in confidence that Sir J. May embarks tomorrow for Lisbon to relieve Webber Smith, who, report says, has displeased His Grace.

He takes out a detachment of sixty men, and forty horses are selected to follow when the vessel is ready to receive them. I only knew of May's going an hour ago. He is far from well, and therefore it is possible may not be able to retain it. I mention this as a *confidential hint* to you, for if anything caused his removal I guess where a successor would be sought for.

Ever yours,
With our united regards,
In haste to save post,
W. Bull.

A letter from the late General Parker explains more fully the grounds of Colonel Webber Smith's recall:—

Woolwich,
February 10, 1827.

It is quite possible Hardinge may have written to you from London that Webber Smith is recalled from his command and May appointed to supersede him, and embarks from hence this day. You know the state of the equipment which lately left our shores, and with your experience will not be surprised at hearing Smith, so soon as he landed, began by making some little changes. It however appears, from what I have been able to collect, that he did not stop there, but like a *Radical* went earnestly to work to restore things to what we have hitherto considered an efficient state; with which object in view he at once broke up the ball cartridge brigade and gave the 9-prs. and 24-

131

pr. howitzers eight horses, and I believe even drafted the men of the company attached to the carts to the brigades.

I conclude, however, all this must have received the sanction of Sir W. Clinton. Be that as it may, so soon as the news reached the Ordnance Office, His Grace's wrath was excited, and he ordered him at once to be relieved. Before any judgment is passed, it is but fair to both parties to hear all the *pro's* and *con's*, which we must delay till the arrival of Webber.

The following letter on the same subject is from Sir Augustus Frazer:—

Woolwich,
February 12, 1827.

My dear Ross,

I seldom write to you, both because I am a good deal occupied, and because we have rarely any corps news worth communicating. I have now two pieces of news, both of which you will regret to hear.

The first is the death, on Friday the 9th inst., of our good old commandant, General Ramsay, who had been ailing for a few days, owing to an accident to his finger by the slamming of a door; and this sudden death was, till within a very few hours, altogether unexpected. As a very honest, just man, he will long be regretted. It is of course too early yet to suppose which of our major-generals may be appointed his successor. The general opinion balances between Wood and Fisher.

My next news, which is universally regretted, is the recall from Portugal of Webber Smith, who has been superseded by May. He sailed yesterday for Lisbon, in a transport carrying out sixty gunners, as an augmentation of fifteen men to each of the four companies already in Portugal. Smith embarked in the last days of December, with four companies—Wylde's, Wilgress's, Taylor's, and Bridges'. These companies were attached to three field batteries of four pieces each, and to a musket ball cartridge division. The equipment received the duke's sanction, and allowed six horses per 9-pr. gun, and four horses per wagon, making sixty-five horses per battery.

The horses—which included those of Dyneley's and Elliot's Troops—were all young and good; the drivers were such men as were supposed in the companies to be best fitted for that duty. Two of the batteries having been ordered from Lisbon to move to Abrantes and Elvas, and the third being ordered to be in readiness to move, Webber Smith, fearing the known difficulties of the country, broke up the original equipment, horsed his guns with eight horses and his wagons with six, mounting his officers and non-commissioned officers on country horses, and getting mules for the transport of his musket ball cartridges.

This departure from the equipment originally determined by the duke has drawn down His Grace's displeasure, and the consequence has been that May has superseded Webber Smith. May's health has for some time been very considerably restored, but he is still far from well—indeed I fear very unequal to exertion of mind or body. His orders are to restore the original equipment. (The expedition to Portugal returned to England at the end of about twelve months, without the efficiency of its equipments having been tested by active service.)

Richard Jones has bought about 70 young horses since Webber Smith sailed; he has been authorised to purchase as far as 200. The two troops of Horse Artillery which were dismounted have not received any horses, but shortly will get 30 each. 40 young horses are held in readiness to be sent as a remount to Portugal.

Sir Hew Ross was appointed a magistrate for the county of Cumberland in March, 1828.

The following letter was from the late Lieut.-General Sir Henry Bouverie, on his appointment to the command of the northern district, in succession to Lord Strafford:—

Tadcaster,
August 1, 1828.

My dear Sir,

I desired Major Wood to communicate to you my wish that everything may be conducted in the corps under your care in the same manner as it has been during the reign of my predecessor in this command. I am anxious, however, to express to you the satisfaction which I feel at finding the artillery in your hands, and I beg you to feel assured that I shall at all times have the greatest pleasure in contributing as far as in my power to your comfort and convenience.

I cannot consult that of the corps under your command better than by leaving them as much as possible to you.

Believe me,
My dear Sir,
Ever very sincerely yours,
(Signed)   H. D. Bouverie,
Major-General.

Lt.-Col. Sir H. Ross, &c., &c, &c.

The disturbed state of the manufacturing districts at the period of the Reform. agitation made the position of a commanding officer in the northern district one of unusual responsibility, and the following letter from Sir Henry Bouverie to Sir Hew Ross contains such clear instructions for the guidance of officers in times of disturbance, that it will well repay perusal:—

Aldwarke, Saturday Evening,
October 16, 1831.

My dear Ross,

I have received your letters of the 12th and 15th. I am glad to find that you feel yourself more at ease, and trust that when the arrangements are completed, the country will be secured against all mischief. We shall have a strong force at Newcastle, and if the government allow the 60th to proceed to Carlisle and the neighbourhood, no fear need I imagine be entertained. I have only time to answer your question in a general way.

1st. No troops must be employed unless upon the requisition of a magistrate, and in his presence, upon any account whatever.

2nd. If any attack is made upon troops, it must be repelled *vi et armis,* with or without the concurrence or assistance of the civil power.

3rd. The utmost caution must at all times be observed, and the greatest care taken to prevent any collision between the troops and the people. No insult, however gross, short of actual violence, must be allowed as an excuse for military interference. Patience is as essentially the duty of a soldier at home as it is under a cannonade.

4th. I would not have you billet cavalry in the town of Carlisle. They can always march ten miles to their stables, and I would never if I could avoid it use cavalry without infantry to support them; if you do, they will get you into a scrape.

It is better that troops should march ten miles to secure and quiet quarters than be ill at ease, in consequence of being nearer; this, however, must in all cases be regulated by circumstances and your own discretion, in which, however little confidence you may feel, I feel the greatest. I am very glad to find that Major Hughes is acting so judiciously; pray tell him so. The artillery will be with you immediately, the provisions not so soon; the detachment from the Isle of Man, I should hope in a very few days.

Yours sincerely,

H. Bouverie.

I am very glad that you think of attending the Quarter Sessions at Penrith. I see no reason for making any secret of what is known of the state of this country, or that government is in possession of the information, or that troops are marching into the district.

H. B.

The following letter was addressed to Sir Alexander Dickson, applying for the temporary assistance of Captain, afterwards Major Bridges, as a staff officer, on account of the state of the district:—

Confidential.

Stonehouse,
October 31, 1830.

My dear Dickson,

Your sources of information are such that I have not thought of troubling you with any account of the alarm that has for some time prevailed in and around Carlisle, in common with other parts of this manufacturing country, from the widely extended union that has taken place, and the daring manner in which they have avowed their object; the position, however, in which I am now placed leads me to allude to it, and to appeal to your friendship for advice and assistance.

Sir H. Bouverie, from whom I have always experienced the greatest kindness and confidence, lately wrote to me to say that he found his hands so full, watching the more populous and southern part of his district, that he wished I would allow him to consider me as a brigadier in this northern part of it; and he directed all the troops stationed in the counties of Northumberland, Durham, Cumberland, and Westmoreland, and in the town of Lancaster and the towns in Lancashire to the north thereof, to send me returns of their strength, and to be held ready to move upon my order.

I candidly stated, in my answer to the general, that I felt the greatest diffidence in my own powers and experience to undertake so great a responsibility; but as he has repeated the assurance of his confidence, and the order is given, there is nothing left for me but to do the best I can to discharge the important duties that may devolve on me, though I hope and believe that here we shall not be disturbed, as, from the best information I can collect, disaffection and combination are as yet but partial, and confined to the worst class of weavers and others.

The castle is already made secure by having a sufficient garrison, and a regiment of infantry is on the march to be cantoned in the neighbourhood of Carlisle, and the general intends to send his assistant quartermaster-general to see them settled in quarters; but as I dread the risk of inconvenience to the troops and the ill consequences that might follow any mal-arrangement of routes, returns, &c, to which my inexperience in the movement of them might give rise, I requested to have the assistance of a staff officer, but as I have received no answer, I suppose I am to be left to struggle on as I can.

In this dilemma it has occurred to me that Bridges might, if he is willing to favour me so far, and not disagreeable to himself, render me the service I want. I am not sufficiently acquainted with him to form an opinion myself, but knowing that he enjoys your friendship and that he has been much with you, I am prepared to expect that he is capable of rendering me all the assistance I can require, either at the desk or in the field, should it unfortunately be required.

Should you think him the man I have supposed, and would kindly prevail with him to come and take up his abode with me instead of joining his troop at Newcastle, until we see whether or not the present unsatisfactory state of things may not pass away, you would do me the greatest kindness. At present my situation is most embarrassing. A considerable force, widely dispersed over the country I have described, is placed at my disposal; I am told this neighbourhood is the point of especial jealousy on the part of government, and the city of Carlisle so much so as to be considered unsafe to billet troops in; and I am left without the assistance of any officer capable from ability or experience to aid me, in the event of being obliged to put that force in motion.

I need not add that I shall be anxious for your answer, or that in the event of my plan answering, I shall do all and everything in my power to make Bridges comfortable whilst he gives me the pleasure of his company.

The general writes me two of the 24-pr. howitzers are already at Chester, and the other two he expects will arrive tomorrow at Manchester. He gives an unsatisfactory account of that neighbourhood, but feels himself strong and ready for the worst that may come. I hope the display of so large a force as is, or soon will be, assembled in the manufacturing country, will check disturbance, or at all events enable him to put it down with a strong hand. The tranquillity of this neighbourhood will, I think, depend much on what may take place in Lancashire.

Yours, &c,

H. D. Ross.

Sir A. Dickson's reply to this letter was as follows:—

Woolwich,
November 5, 1830.

My dear Ross,

I don't know a more efficient officer in His Majesty's service than Capt. Bridges, or one more likely to be useful to you in the manner you describe; and in mentioning him as a perfect gentleman and pleasant companion, there is no person better qualified than myself to name him as meriting the most implicit confidence, as he is the most intimate friend I have in the world.

He would be glad to do anything in which he could make himself useful, and he is truly grateful for your favourable views towards him. He therefore will be most happy to join you after the 24th, or earlier if it was indispensable, though it would inconvenience him much; but he very properly observed it would be requisite he should join the troop, in case sickness or any other cause should incapacitate Major Dyneley; and of course he would equally do so as soon as his assistance was unnecessary to you.

The letters which follow were written to Sir Henry Bouverie:—

To Major-General Sir Henry Bouverie, K.C.B.

Carlisle,
November, 5, 1830.

I have looked over the informations against the men referred to. The assault was certainly a brutal one, and some of those attacked are a good deal hurt; but as four of the rioters are already committed for further examination, and the others soon may, I hope the affair may pass off quietly. The cause of the disturbance, I understand, grew out of a strike on the part of Mr. ——'s spinners for wages. That point was settled by his agreeing to give the same as the other mills did; but Mr.—— having engaged some new hands during the dispute, the old ones insist on their being turned off before they return to their work, and hence the disturbance. Mr. N. tells me he believes a negotiation is still going on, and he hopes an accommodation may be brought about.

Mr. —— is anxious to get a guard of soldiers to protect his mill, but I have declared it to be impossible, and advised Mr. N. to inform him that he ought to take measures to protect his own property; and besides I do not see anything in the information to shew there is an intention on the part of his former workmen to injure it. The mill is situated at ——, about five miles from hence, and of course beyond the city or police authority.

I shall of course not move a man unless called upon by the magistrates, and I do not think there will be any such call made.

I yesterday heard from Lord Lonsdale:—'I thought it advisable to ascertain what force of yeomanry could be assembled at a short notice, and I find that there are upwards of 100 may be easily assembled in this neighbourhood. Any notice sent to this place (Lowther) will be attended to.'

I received yours of the 2nd yesterday, for which I thank you. I hope Dickson will make the arrangement I have proposed, which will render any other unnecessary as to my having an officer from another corps.

Ever yours faithfully,

H. D. Ross.

Should it be absolutely necessary to call in aid, would it be proper for me to order the 91st from Langholm instead of sending to Newcastle? The former is only eighteen miles, the other fifty-six.

To the same.
<u>Private</u>.

Carlisle,
November 10, 1830.

I have received yours of the 8th, and I rejoice to find that your accounts from Lancashire are so satisfactory. I wish I could gratify you with a similar report from hence, but I am sorry to say there have been doings here the last two evenings that may, though I hope they will not, lead to mischief. About seven o'clock on Monday evening, a few men from Caldew Gate, followed by a rabble of boys and women, proceeded to the Market Cross, carrying an effigy of the Duke of Wellington, which they burnt; after which they retired, and all was quiet at eight o'clock, and so continued.

Last night, about the same time, similar honour was paid to Mr. Peel, proceeding from the same quarter, but more numerously attended; and after the ceremony was concluded, amidst cheering, they withdrew as before without any disturbance. Here the matter I hope may rest, but it is reported they mean to repeat the scene tonight. I trust it will prove otherwise, for such proceedings being allowed to go on with impunity may be repeated once too often. In the meantime, the civil powers have taken no steps to interfere, and do not show any uneasiness about them.

As a set off to what I have just stated, I have great pleasure in telling you that I have just received a note from Mr. Nanson to say, 'Messrs. ———'s cotton-spinners are gone to work today at ———; and more have applied to be taken on there at night, in consequence of their mills in Carlisle not being at work. They are prevented at present, on account of some alterations they are making in the machinery.' I am very glad that this matter is settled, as I should have felt great reluctance to sending any men to ———, as to go there it is necessary to pass through Caldew and Shaddon Gates, which might have led to trouble.

Private.

Carlisle,
November 20, 1830.

Since my last letter everything has remained quiet here, if I except a procession that took place on Thursday evening, when, according to Mr. Nanson's opinion, about 3000 people, consisting not of the rabble that infested the streets on the former occasions, but of the lower classes generally, paraded through the streets with music and flags (the northern union and tri-coloured), and several placards, such as "Peace to the City, " "Radical Reform," "Death to the Wellington Administration," &c, with the usual accompaniment of torches. Having gone through the city, they separated quietly.

Mr. N. tells me he had information of their intended proceedings, but as he also ascertained that they were intended to be quite peaceable, although they would be prepared to use force if opposed, it was thought advisable to let them pass unmolested; because in the first place the object of their meeting was understood to be solely the expression of joy at the change of administration, and likewise from the numbers assembled, there appeared no hope of the constables being able to interfere with any good effect.

There has been a meeting of the magistrates again this morning, when they were of opinion that the character and notions of the people appearing to be changed, they hope there is no longer any danger of disturbance, and under present circumstances they consider it the wisest policy not to irritate them by any display of hostility to their boasted triumph. I thought it right not to attend the meeting, but I have since learnt what I have stated from some of the magistrates who were present.

Mr. N. informs me further, that after tonight, when there is to be a similar assemblage at Dalston to that held here on Thursday last, as a return for the attendance of the Dalston people on that night, there is no present intention of repeating such doings. I hope it will prove so; for most assuredly the oftener they are, the less likely they are to be discontinued, and mischief may at last ensue. Nothing could be more orderly than their conduct, which Mr. N. says he expected, as his information stated that they were directed to be provided with arms or sticks in case of being resisted, but that peace was their desire, and individuals even were appointed amongst them to prevent boys and others from doing anything that could lead to a different result.

I hope the threatened difference between the masters and their workmen in Lancashire has been settled. Did I venture to offer an opinion on politics, it would be sorrow for the loss of the duke, to guide us in these stormy times—for himself, as I cannot envy the man who succeeds to his high office, so I think he may find something to reconcile him to the loss of it.

Carlisle,
December 1, 1830.

I am sorry to inform you that last night, between nine and ten o'clock, two stacks were set on fire, one of corn the other hay, close to the town though at different places, and I have read the deposition of a very respectable inhabitant, who states that he, with some others, had succeeded in extinguishing the fire of the latter, when they were interrupted by the people, who had till then been looking quietly on, in consequence of an individual exclaiming, 'It is the *swing* system; let it burn!' which was immediately cheered, the line of water-carriers broken, and those who were on the stack, throwing the smoking hay off, were driven from it.

A summons was issued this forenoon for the assembly of the neighbouring magistrates, and they are at this moment sitting; but as it is near post hour, I fear I shall not have it in my power to send you the result of their deliberations tonight.

My object, therefore, in giving you this information, is to prepare you for a demand on their part for some cavalry; and as you told me the dragoons were likely to march from Newcastle into Scotland, I fear you will find it difficult to comply with their request, and until I hear from you I shall not take upon myself to send orders, lest I should interfere with some more important demand for them, even should they not yet have marched. I will send you the result of the magistrates' deliberation tomorrow.

I am sorry to say that in these movements not a symptom of energy has been shown by the police commissioners or civil authorities.

Carlisle,
December 2, 1830.

Shortly after I despatched my letter to you last night, I received a request to attend the magistrates. I found them in consultation with some of the police commissioners, the former urging the necessity of the latter increasing their number of constables, but apparently with little effect. After a great deal of talk to little purpose, I was asked whether it were possible to get a troop of dragoons to be quartered in the town, which they all declared to be the only force to terrify the mob. I replied that I thought it very doubtful, but that I could have no objections to forward any declarations of the opinions and wishes of magistrates to you; at the same time I thought it right to state to them that until they had shown some disposition to protect themselves by embodying and using a suitable body of constables, their application for the protection of more troops would not have the weight it otherwise might reckon upon.

The magistrates met this morning, and received depositions against four individuals who are supposed to have fired the stacks. About twelve o'clock I was sent for, to request I would have the troops ready to support the civil power in an attempt on the part of the constables to seize them. They were kept in readiness to answer any demand of the magistrates until three o'clock, when it was intimated to me that the people having assembled in Caldew Gate, it was determined not to make the attempt, and at the same time the enclosed was put into my hand, and since then I have had a message from the magistrates, that instead of *one* they meant *two* troops, not being aware of the strength of a troop when the letter was written.

I understand the police are to endeavour to seize the men informed against in the night-time, but in truth the lamentable state and character of the civil power is such that nothing but trouble, annoyance, and danger to the peace of the country can grow out of it.

On Tuesday night, when the fires occurred, there was not a magistrate to be found to call out the special constables, or take any means for the preservation of order; the mayor even was absent. It is so far satisfactory that it is supposed only a few were concerned in firing the stacks.

Carlisle,

December 6, 1830.

I am sorry to inform you another stack of corn was burnt last night, or rather in the evening. It was situated by itself, in a field near Dalston. As far as I can learn, there was no attempt made to extinguish the fire, and it burnt out quietly. Your letter of the 4th reached me this morning, and at the same time a communication from Sir James Graham to request me to meet him at twelve o'clock. He told me he had been authorised by Lord Hill to desire me to lend every assistance in my power to enable the magistrates in this county to carry into effect the arrangements for forming a strong constabulary force upon the plan adopted with success in Sussex by the Duke of Richmond.

He laid the whole system before a very large bench of magistrates, and I am happy to say they at once determined upon taking immediate measures to carry it into effect. He also brought with him instructions for swearing in all the pensioners as special constables, and this also is at this moment doing. The addition in this way will be very considerable to the civil force, and as he expressed himself in very strong terms against the employment of the troops, unless in the last resort, I hope I shall not again be called upon for their aid except under very urgent circumstances.

Sir James expressed some anxiety as to the safety of the militia arms at Whitehaven. I explained to him the communication I had with you on that subject, and said I would again mention it to you; though, in fact, as he stated that the staff of the militia are to be armed, I should imagine it might form a sufficient guard. There has been a variety of rumours today of an intended attempt to release the prisoners in the jail, but I have no doubt they are without foundation. As the arrangements consequent on the formation of this new system of police will bring an additional duty upon me, I have called to my assistance Capt. Bridges, of Dyneley's Troop, and who with your leave I will retain here. Should you approve of my doing so, you will oblige me by giving me an authority for so doing, that he may claim travelling expenses from Newcastle. I learn from Sir James that this is a day reported to be looked to with some anxiety, on account of meetings to be held in various places. I hope they will all end quietly.

Carlisle,

December 8, 1830.

I was much gratified to find by your letter of the 6th that you approved of my proceedings here. I have just received your note of the 7th, and I am very sorry to hear that you have found it necessary to move your headquarters. I shall be anxious to know that order is restored at Staleybridge. Although I have actually nothing to tell you of the least importance, I think in these times it will be at any rate satisfactory to you to know that such is the case.

The swearing-in of the special constables is now going on, and I have no doubt will have an excellent effect. The country people appear to enter into the spirit of the system with good heart, and where there are active magistrates and intelligent leaders, I am sure it must work well; but I fear in some cases they are not to be found.

The magistrates were in doubt whether the out-pensioners special constables should be armed or not. Sir James Graham referred it to me. I decidedly objected to it, except with sticks, as I feared the habits of some might lead to an ill use of them.

Sir James requested me to write to the commander-in-chief, to inform him how matters stood here; I have therefore reported by this post to Lord Fitzroy that we are perfectly tranquil at present, and that the swearing-in of the special constables is going on so far prosperously.

To Major-General Lord Fitzroy Somerset.
Private.

Carlisle,
December 8, 1830.

My dear Lord,

Sir James Graham was here on Monday, and conveyed to me the commands of the commander-in-chief that I should give every assistance in my power to the magistrates of this neighbourhood in their endeavours to organise a system of constabulary force similar to that established by the Duke of Richmond, and that his lordship desired I should inform him that progress was making.

I have great pleasure in stating that the necessary arrangements were instantly commenced, and already a considerable number of special constables have been sworn-in in the surrounding country, as well as in the city. Some leaders of sections have been named, and the country people who have been sworn show the best disposition to enter upon their duties; so that I think in a few days there will be a considerable force of this description, with a heart and good will to protect their property.

It is gratifying to me to be able to inform your lordship that at present we are perfectly tranquil, and my private information leads me to believe that there is not any movement in view at this moment, nor do I believe there ever would be in this city were the police placed on a proper footing.

I have on a former occasion stated my opinion on this subject to Sir H. Bouverie, but if I may be allowed, I could wish to press upon your attention that there is but one mode of procuring the peace of the city, which is by taking the power out of the hands of about fifty commissioners who now use it unworthily, and giving it to *one,* who should be a stipendiary magistrate, as is the case at Manchester.

I so stated my opinion to Sir J. Graham, who appeared to acquiesce in it.

The following are extracts from Sir Henry Bouverie's replies to these letters:—

Aldwerke,
November 14, 1830.

My dear Ross,

I am very much obliged to you for your very satisfactory communication. If the magistrates will but be firm, they will be able to keep all things quiet. I am particularly pleased with the tone which you took in speaking to them; it was precisely what was right. I regret to say that meetings are taking place in all the villages about Staleybridge, &c., and that the most violent language is held; they are preparatory to a great meeting of operatives, which is to be held at Ashton Moss or Hough Hill, on I do not know what day.

Rotherham,
December 2, 1830.

I am extremely sorry to find that the '*swing* system' is beginning in your neighbourhood. I hope that the magistrates will be alert, and act with vigour, or they and others will suffer very severely inevitably. . . . I wish you, however, to *take an early opportunity* of stating to the magistrates that it (a squadron of cavalry at Newcastle) can only be employed *in aid* of the civil power, and that therefore, unless they themselves act, the troops cannot.

They should immediately swear in a strong constabulary force in the neighbourhood, and take such other measures as are taken in other parts of the country. . . . Should you require infantry, the 82nd depot is available, but I wish you not to quarter it in any town unless it can be billeted close together, and if the authorities will not engage for that, you have my orders not to move it. . . . The great object should be

144

to make the magistrates, and civil power exert itself, and to give them assistance, but never to move a man without positive requisition; and, in short, to keep the troops as quiet as possible.

Aldwarke,

December 5, 1830.

Your very satisfactory letter of the 4th reached me, and I congratulate you on the prospect of tranquillity it holds out. I beg that you will not feel for an instant that you give me any 'trouble;' it is delightful to me to have it proved by your letters and conduct that you understand me, and that we agree so perfectly as we do upon all points. It is most agreeable to me to have such a coadjutor. Your arrangement of the troops for the apprehension of the incendiaries was everything that I could wish; it ensured success had the people been found, or had there been any opposition to the civil power, and they were so placed as to be out of risk of check or insult.

I trust that Sir James Graham will be able to give a good account of you when he returns to London, which he left, as I understand, under some fears of what he might find upon his arrival at Netherby.

Sir Henry Bouverie having requested Sir Hew Ross to ascertain how matters stood at Newcastle, in consequence of a turn-out of the colliers, and a fear that the keelmen and sailors would also be discontented, he made the following reports on the subject:—

Newcastle-upon-Tyne,

April 2, 1831.

My dear General,

I arrived here last night, and I have today endeavoured to gain information respecting the state of this part of the country.

It appears that it is customary for the pitmen to engage by the year with the coal-owners; a part of them completed their time this day, and ought to re-enter on Tuesday, but it is understood they are determined not to do so, and in one or two instances they have threatened those who have.

The remainder will complete their engagement on Tuesday, and in like manner they also will not re-engage, and the whole, both from the Wear and Tyne, are to assemble on the moor here on Wednesday, to consult and be bound to support each other. The owners' committee have offered certain terms, but they do not come up to the demands of the pitmen, and are rejected, and the owners say they cannot agree to those of the pitmen.

It is difficult to form an opinion as to how it will end, but there appears a very strong one that the latter have been hardly dealt with, and that a timely and liberal treatment on the part of the owners might have prevented the present state of things. I attended a meeting of the county magistrates today: present—Sir Charles Clavering, Mr. Brandling of Gosforth, Mr. Collingwood, Mr. Dixon, Major Lawson, and others, and they were all agreed in their wish to have a troop of dragoons here, and expressed great surprise at the one having been sent hence to Houghton-le-Spring; especially as they (the magistrates) did not ask for it, and they consider it wanted as much here as it can be there.

I told them that I had no doubt it would be immediately replaced, with which they seemed content. Should the pitmen continue long out of work, it will throw idle, in addition to their own number (about 30,000), several thousand keelmen and sailors, and it is incalculable the mischief they may do if they follow up their threats to burn the pits and to destroy the machinery. Should you approve of a troop coming here from Leeds, I would suggest that the one at Houghton-le-Spring should return here and the former take its place there. That arrangement would enable a troop to arrive here a day sooner, and when quiet is restored, the former might go back to Leeds.

Newcastle-upon-Tyne,
April 3, 1831.

Nothing has transpired today that I have heard respecting the pitmen, and I have only to add to the information contained in my letter of yesterday, that the mayor expresses great anxiety for the state of disorder that may be produced on the river amongst the keelmen and sailors should the usual supply of coals be long withheld.

He also told me he had made an application to the Secretary of State to have a naval force placed in the river, as well as more troops here, and he let me see the answer. It takes no notice of the former, and refers him to you on the latter point. I told him it was probable he would soon have a troop of dragoons here, which appeared to give him satisfaction.

★★★★★★

Similar fears were entertained, in August 1831, of disturbances in the neighbourhood of Whitehaven, and troops were moved into that district on the requisition of the civil authorities, to ensure order. In October of the same year, Sir Henry Bouverie writes to inform Sir

Hew that he finds from Lord Fitzroy Somerset that considerable anxiety is felt as to what effect may be produced in the north by what the Lords may do with the Reform Bill, and that he had been desired to pay particular attention to Carlisle.

The following are extracts from Sir Hew Ross's replies and further reports:—

To Sir Henry Bouverie.

Carlisle,
October 4, 1831.

My dear General,

I have received your letters of the 1st and 2nd, and I am happy to inform you that from the information I can collect, there does not appear the least reason to apprehend riot or disturbance here in consequence of the divisions that may take place in the House of Lords on the Reform Bill. This I have understood for some time past has been the general feeling; and on the receipt of your letter this morning, I came over to make more particular enquiries, and I learn from my former source of intelligence, as well as from other well-informed quarters, that such is still the feeling, and that even the Radical Committee have not made any effort to rouse their party. I have put myself in communication with those who are likely to give me good information, and you may rely on being apprised of anything that comes to my knowledge.

Carlisle,
October 10, 1831.

The result of the division in the House of Lords, upon being known here this morning, produced a call for a meeting by the Reform Committee, on the race course, at one o'clock. It took place at one o'clock, and has just separated at three in the most orderly manner. The object was to express regret at the bill being lost, and all the speeches were, I understand, very peaceable. I am led to believe that there is no intention of any attempt being made to promote anything like riot or disturbance; but before sending the troop of the Bays back to their quarters, I have thought it safest to ascertain the opinion of the magistrates, and with this view I have requested Mr. Nanson, the town clerk, to write to me on the subject on Wednesday, so that if all remains quiet, the troop may proceed on its march on Thursday or Friday. By that time also I shall have heard from you; but in the event of Mr. Nanson's letter being favourable, I will not wait for your instructions, as you may have left Manchester before this can reach you.

Carlisle,
October 13, 1831.

I am sorry to inform you that we are not likely to remain so quiet here as my letter of Monday last must have led you to expect.

On Thursday evening the mob, taking the hint from some of the speakers at the meeting the day before, paraded the streets in a tumultuous manner, and finished by burning the bishop in effigy, in the midst of the most diabolical execrations and threats against him and his residence at Rose Castle; and I am sorry to say he has had several letters from gentlemen in Carlisle begging him to be upon his guard, as they have reason to fear that there are some of the people ready to carry their threats into execution. In consequence of this information, his lordship last night wrote to ask me, in the event of an attack, what assistance he might expect from the troops; to which I replied, to the utmost of my means, and immediately sent orders to Major Kelly to be prepared to do so.

I have just returned from calling on him at Rose Castle, and having explained to him how I am situated as to force, we have agreed that it is best not to take any other measures in the first instance than those I have named—*viz.*, Major Kelly to be ready to send a party should it be necessary; and in the meantime he is taking the precaution to arm, and keep a constant watch with his own establishment and neighbours.

From what I have stated, as well as other indications of a mischievous spirit, I shall not for the present part with the dragoons from Brampton. Should these threats continue, would you think it advisable to quarter a sergeant's party at Rose Castle until things become more quiet? I am inclined to think it might be as safe a plan as risking the marching of a party of eighty men through a disaffected and populous country to his assistance, in the event of actual attack. More I think it would be unsafe to part with from the castle, and it must be always remembered that the 24th are all boys, and hardly half drilled.

I should mention that the bishop is averse to having troops out, unless in case of absolute necessity, and he would much rather trust his defence to his own people, could he find the means of arming them. Would it be proper for me to supply any from the Ordnance Depots, should he desire it?

Being in haste, I shall only add that I learn from Mr. Nanson, who

I have just seen, that although there is no accounting for the violence that may be perpetrated by an infuriated mob, he has no reason to believe that any organised plan for the destruction of property has been adopted as yet, and he still hopes there will not, though he hears it has been talked of among them.

I am glad to hear you remain so peaceable at Manchester, and I hear the same of Glasgow.

★★★★★★

Sir Henry Bouverie replied that there could be no objection to the bishop having a serjeant and ten or twelve steady men sent if he wished it to Rose Castle, nor to his receiving arms and ammunition in the manner ordered by the ordnance to be observed in Lancashire, and as is done at Manchester and in the neighbourhood, and at this moment at Lord Wilton's, Lord Balcarras', &c.

★★★★★★

Stonehouse,
October 22, 1831.

I received your letter of the 19th, and by the same post one from the Bishop of Carlisle to inform me that he had procured a sufficient supply of firearms for his people, and that he hoped the safety of Rose Castle was secured, unless some new excitement was raised. In that case he had made arrangements for instant application to be made to the magistrates in Carlisle, who would call for assistance from the troops; and as Major Kelly has received instructions from me, I have no doubt he will give it effectually. Rose Castle is about seven miles from Carlisle, and unfortunately in the worst possible situation, being three miles beyond Dalston, and I am sorry to say there is not a place on that side of Carlisle at all calculated to contain the dragoons.

I had myself thought, had it been possible, that it would be desirable to quarter them in that neighbourhood, and mentioned it to the bishop; but I found without the troop was widely dispersed in a very dangerous country, it was quite impracticable. The bishop returned to Stanwick, near Darlington, on Tuesday. He was only at Rose to see how the building was going on, the house not yet being fit to receive his family; but hearing of the threats against him by the mob from Mr. Mounsey, the son of his registrar and a member of the Committee of the Reform Association, he stayed until he saw it in a state capable of making a defence should it be attacked.

Since my last letter there has not been anything like riot, but I understand, as during last year, there have been considerable assemblages of people at night in Caldew Gate; and it is said they have with difficulty been dissuaded from repeating their processions and burnings by their leaders, under the influence of the Association.

Whether that body may be able to maintain their power is doubtful. I hope they may; otherwise such doings must lead to mischief.

On Thursday I had a visit from the mayor of Carlisle, who, after consulting with his colleagues, came to ask me to quarter the dragoons in the city, saying that should any disturbance take place he has no hope of offering any resistance to a mob, except by calling out the troops.

I told him there was but one way of obtaining his request—providing good and secure quarters and stabling in one, or at most two, buildings or yards. He declared that he had no means of doing so, and so he must be content that things remain as they are; but he urged the necessity of not parting with the dragoons from Brampton for the present, and I comforted him with the assurance that I hoped the troop would remain there, at least until the present excitement had passed away.

He told me he had received a letter from the Home Office, calling upon him to communicate with the commanding officer of the troops, and to take every precaution to preserve the peace of the city, and to afford protection to the bishop and his property. He has also received a copy of the new act for the appointment of special constables; but knowing what you do of the mal-administration of the civil establishments of Carlisle, I think you will not be surprised when I express great doubt of their having nerve to carry the law into effect by calling upon the householders to be sworn; and in truth it is not much to be wondered at, considering the system of intimidation that has been so long practised, and the dread the people have of becoming unpopular with the mob.

I went yesterday to enquire what is to be done, but I found nothing had been decided.

Not feeling sure, from the P.S. to your letter, that you wish me to communicate with the commanding officer of the Westmoreland Yeomanry, I have refrained from doing so, and the more so as I have not been able to obtain any information that would show it to be urgently necessary. I am therefore unwilling, by doing so prematurely, to risk an uncalled-for alarm.

Should you, however, think it desirable, I shall with pleasure write to him, to request he will hold his corps ready. I will thank you to desire Colonel Thorn to send me some blank routes, as those I had were employed in the late movement of troops to Whitehaven, &c Colonel Power informed me some time ago that he feared mischief was brewing at Newcastle, but not having heard lately I was in hopes he was deceived.

Carlisle,
November 5, 1831.

I am happy to say everything has remained quiet here since my last letter, but I regret to add that I this morning received a note as follows from Mr. N.:— 'The posture of affairs here, since the dreadful outrages at Bristol, is such as to make it necessary to pause before the cavalry force is removed from Brampton.' I have just seen him and the mayor, by whom I was informed that although they have not ascertained that any positive plan is in agitation, they have certain information that, since the proceedings at Bristol, the violent party amongst the manufacturers and others have held the most outrageous language, and are only restrained at present by the Association, with whom they are very angry for opposing their wishes to make an example of some of their supposed enemies by burning their houses.

The county meeting is to take place on the 15th, and probably a good deal will depend on the temper of the speakers on that occasion; for I think there is no doubt as to the disposition of the rabble to act promptly, if roused to mischief.

The bishop, I have just heard, is returned to Rose Castle, with the intention of consecrating a new church lately built in Caldew Gate; but I understand the dean and clergy, and some of the magistrates, have sent a request to him to postpone the ceremony, which I hope he will do, as it would inevitably produce insult and riot.

I am decidedly of opinion that it would be a great advantage to have some carbines issued to the troops of Horse Artillery. Circumstanced as this district is at present, they would be a great security when on a march alone, as frequently must happen to the troops, and add to the safety of the barracks they occupy, and I shall be very glad if you think it advisable."

Stonehouse,
November 9, 1831.

I have received yours of yesterday, and although I have nothing new to communicate, I think in these anxious times you will be glad to hear that it is so. I yesterday found the magistrates at Carlisle in considerable agitation, in consequence of the reported riots at Preston. They were uneasy about the jail; I therefore made arrangements with them and Major Kelly that in the event of their seeing any necessity for it, a guard of nine men should be placed there, and that Major K. shall be at all times ready to give them effectual aid if called upon. I likewise gave him authority, should he at any time see occasion for it, at once to send an express to Brampton for the dragoons; and I have directed Capt. Copland to give immediate attention to the order, sending at the same time an orderly to apprise me that he has done so.

Thus, I hope we shall be ready for anything that may occur, and I trust, in the midst of your many cares, you may feel in some measure at ease with regard to us. As I have no report today from Carlisle, I conclude all is right; I intend to go there tomorrow, and if there is anything new you shall know it. I write in haste to save the Brampton post.

The following was Sir Henry Bouverie's reply to the last letter:—

Blyth,
November 11, 1831.

My dear Ross,

I rejoice to see that you are peaceable at Carlisle. The satisfactory accounts from Leeds, and the very prompt manner in which the disturbances at Coventry have been put down by the civil power and the military under Colonel Ewart, will I think give us some breathing time. I shall have a squadron of the 2nd Dragoon Guards at hand, with orders for one troop to obey your orders in case of your sending for it, and I beg you will not scruple to send for it if you want it.

I have sent an order to Chester for 25 stand of carbines, with belts and pouches, to be sent to each troop of artillery, the board having sanctioned the issue. I think that that number will be sufficient for the purpose, and will not encumber them by loading all their dismounted men; if you think that they are too many, the supplies can easily be returned into store at some future occasion.

I trust that the cholera, if cholera it be, or whatever disease it is, will not extend beyond Sunderland, but the accounts are very distressing.

Yours sincerely,

H. Bouverie.

On the 19th November, Sir Hew Ross was able to report that a county meeting which had excited uneasiness had passed off quietly, and that everything looked so peaceable that he should order back a troop of cavalry which had been detached from Newcastle, and which he had authority to detain through the winter.

Sir Henry Bouverie's desire for a supply of carbines for the Horse Artillery was fully concurred in by Sir Hew Ross, and after communicating with the commanding officers of batteries in his district, he recommended that the number should be fixed at twelve per troop or battery. The Horse Artillery and field batteries in England were at this period on a most reduced establishment, without even one ammunition wagon, and Sir Hew Ross addressed the following letter on the subject to Sir H. Bouverie:—

Stonehouse,
November 28, 1831.

My dear General,

Although bad as the times are, I am very unwilling to suppose a case where a greater expenditure of ammunition might be required than the proportions carried with the troops of Horse Artillery and Power's demi-battery, but as the question has been suggested to me by the officers commanding them, I think I do right in naming the subject to you. Cobbe's troop carries 46 rounds, Dyneley's 43, and Power's demi-battery 50, being from 22 to 25 rounds to each gun. That quantity certainly would not last long, if the service of artillery should unfortunately be required in earnest, but that is a matter for your consideration.

Power reports to me that Colonel Holloway has succeeded in rendering the magazine at Newcastle fit for the reception of ammunition, and supposing a case (an impossible one I hope) of having his communication with Tynemouth interrupted, proposes having a reserve of 100 rounds placed there; and the Horse Artillery in like manner are looking to the difficulty of having their expenditure supplied.

Of the necessity of taking every precaution, of course neither they nor I can have any knowledge; but having mentioned the subject, I think I should state what (supposing any arrangement desirable) appears to me the best. To placing ammunition in the magazines, there are these objections: the troops might be removed to a distance from them, and at times they might be left without a proper guard; but I think there can be none to each troop and the "D" Battery being supplied with an ammunition wagon, as is the case with Tweedie's battery at Manchester; and should there be any objection to their being horsed on account of expense, they might when required be moved with hired or pressed horses.

I must again repeat that of the necessity I do not pretend to have an opinion, but I am anxious you should know the proper zeal felt by these officers, and the disappointment they would feel if, after having expended their ammunition, they should find themselves obliged to become quiet spectators of what might be going on.

I have not yet heard that the carbines have reached the troops, but I believe it will be found that they cannot make good use of more than 15 or 16 with each, I hear of nothing but quiet in this neighbourhood at present.

Believe me,

Yours most truly,

H. D. Ross.

Sir Henry Bouverie's reply to this letter was followed by an official application to Sir Alexander Dickson, Deputy-Adjutant-General of Artillery, and the wagons asked for were given—*viz.* one for each troop of Horse Artillery of two guns, and one for a demi field battery at Newcastle, of the same number of guns. By the following letter it would appear that no horses had been given, and that post-horses were to be relied on for their movement:—

Stonehouse,

December 19, 1831.

My dear General,

I return Lord Fitzroy's letter, with many thanks. I shall take care to instruct the officers commanding troops of Horse Artillery as to the manner in which post-horses are to be used, when it is necessary to employ them for the purpose of moving their carriages. With a view to that object, I have requested that wheel harness may be sent with the ammunition wagons. The decision of the master-general respecting the forges is what I expected, because they have always been considered a necessary part of the equipment of field artillery, and in the Horse Artillery to be, with the workmen and tools, as little as possible separated from the troops.

There cannot be a difficulty in carrying the number of carbines now to be, with the troops, and if the swords are found an encumbrance, they shall be carried as you suggest on a march.

I am sorry to hear from Power that the cholera appears to be making steady progress, and he fears it is spreading to the neighbouring villages.

I spoke to Major Kelly this morning about trying to get all his people into the barracks in the event of its showing itself in Carlisle, but I fear it is impossible. He appears to feel more anxiety at his hospital being in the town; but it is too late to find any remedy to meet the present occasion, though it strikes me it might be a favourable opportunity to point out the inconvenience of not having one in the castle.

Yours, &c.,

H. D. R.

Sir Henry Bouverie having referred a communication from the Board of Ordnance on the subject of the carbine equipment to Sir Hew Ross, received the following reply:—

January 28, 1832.

I have received a similar communication from our adjutant-general respecting the proposed equipment of carbines for the troops of Horse Artillery to that stated in Mr. Byham's letter, together with a lecture for having omitted to report to him for the information of the master-general that you had authorised me to return thirteen of the number originally issued to each troop to Mr. Henderson—a form which at the time did not occur to me to be necessary, as I thought the storekeeper's report of the order to receive them would be sufficient.

I am fully aware of your motive in wishing to arm a portion of the dismounted men, and I am quite satisfied that circumstances may arise any day to render their being in possession of carbines of the greatest importance; but as to the mode of carrying them (the carbines), I do not think it is a matter of any consequence to the object you have in view; for in the event of being called upon to act without the support of infantry or cavalry, the officer commanding the troop would of course put the carbines into the hands of the dismounted men, and on all common occasions of march, the manner proposed would certainly be a convenient one for carrying six of them, as the buckets would enable so many to be carried on horseback by the horse-holders without inconvenience, as even in action they are not required to dismount.

The other six, Sir A. Dickson in his letter says should be on the carriages— that is, I presume, on an ordinary march; for in the event of the services of the dismounted men being required, the whole would of necessity be placed in their hands.

Taking this view of the subject, I need not say that I am disposed to think that the arrangements proposed by the deputy-adjutant-general will answer every requisite purpose. I am sorry to hear Dyneley has not taken any carbines with him, as the situation of his park at Mansfield is probably one of those where they are most required for its protection. I shall write to him on the subject.

Yours, &c.,

H. D. Ross.

The approach of the cholera led to the following letter from Sir Hew Ross, on the subject of the hospital and other accommodation for the troops at Carlisle:—

February 25, 1832.

My dear General,

In consequence of receiving a letter from Colonel Holloway to tell me he would be at Carlisle on Friday, I thought it best to defer forming an opinion as to the best means of quartering the outlyers of the 24th Regiment, in the event of the cholera approaching us, until I learnt what plans he contemplated in the castle. I met him yesterday, when he told me he is directed by the master-general to send a report and estimate of cost, &c, of converting the governor's house into a hospital, and providing a permanent quarter for the master gunner in lieu of it, by fitting up one of the buildings used as a store at present for him.

The arrangement I think will be a great improvement, and I suppose not the less desired by the board, as it will save £50 *per annum*, the rent of the present hospital. I took advantage of the opportunity to request Holloway would inspect the different buildings and barracks, with a view to ascertain if it would be possible to fit up temporary accommodation for the outlyers, and he appeared of opinion that it could be effected with ease, and at a trifling cost, and that the only inconvenience would be that the barrack-master would have to pack some old barrack utensils a little closer during the time the buildings should be occupied as barracks.

Colonel Holloway did not say he could make them comfortable barracks, nor should he attempt it, but he thinks the soldiers would be much better so quartered than in the town, should the cholera really make its appearance there. He further said he has no authority to make any such arrangements, nor can he propose it to the board; but should you think it desirable, he will be ready to make a report on the subject.

The arrangements referred to were carried out.

May 20, 1832.—Sir Henry Bouverie writes:—

The ordnance have ordered the light 6-prs. to Hull and Carlisle. Pray tell Major Kelly that I wish the men of his depot to *be* nstructed by the officer of artillery in the gun exercise, &c (without firing); it will make the young ones handy. . . . The master-general has my opinion pretty strongly expressed as to the great improvements which have taken place at Carlisle. Nothing can be quieter than we are here.

In July, 1832, Sir Henry Bouverie forwarded to Sir Hew an urgent application for military assistance from the neighbourhood of Carlisle, which had been made in accordance with a communication from Lord Melbourne through Sir James Graham. Sir Hew's minute on this letter was as follows:—

July 6, 1832.—The magistrates (Mr. Goodenough and Major Wilson) inform me that nothing has transpired in the examinations taken before them that can justify their recommending the Messrs. ——'s request to be complied with.
Communicate to the Messrs. —— the magistrates' opinion, and inform them that if they at any time satisfy the magistrates of the necessity of the case, a guard of a sergeant and 12 men shall be immediately sent to ——, but if they wish to detain them they must provide proper lodgings for them.

H. D. R.

Sir Henry Bouverie left the northern district for Malta in October, 1836, and his opinion of the sound judgment exercised by Sir Hew Ross on this and other occasions was expressed in the following strong terms in his final order to the troops under his command:—

To Colonel Sir Hew Ross, K.C.B., commanding the Royal Artillery, the major-general feels that he is particularly indebted. The manner in which this distinguished corps has behaved, furnishes the strongest proof of the judgment with which it has been commanded; but it is not in that alone that Sir Hew Ross has acquired the strongest claim to the acknowledgment which is now offered to him. In times of great difficulty and discontent, when the peace of the district has been threatened, particularly in the north, disturbance has been mainly kept down by his vigilant superintendence, by his knowledge of the people, and by the high esteem in which his honourable and manly character is held by all ranks.

Sir Hew received also the following letter:—

Delapré Abbey, Northampton,
October 16, 1836.

My dear Ross,

I have taken leave of the district in an order in which I have ventured to use your name in a way much more satisfactory to my own feelings than I can expect it to be to you. I only hope that should the changes and chances of this world again bring us together, that we shall not have forgotten the friendly intercourse which has subsisted between us for so long a period, and that in the meantime, should there be anything in which I can prove the sincerity of my feelings towards you and yours, you will give me an opportunity of doing so.

Yours sincerely and faithfully,

H. D. Bouverie.

The expectation of a brevet which would promote Sir Hew Ross to the regimental rank of colonel, led to his addressing the following letters on the subject to Sir Alexander Dickson and Lord Fitzroy Somerset:—

My dear Dickson,

As the time approaches to which we have been led to look for the completion of the long-talked-of brevet, I am naturally very anxious as to the effect it may produce on my position in the regiment, and although I feel that I have no claim upon your favour to the exclusion of others who may equally hope for your friendly offices on such an occasion, I am sure you will allow me to seek from your friendship such assistance as you may have it in your power to afford me, in the event of being promoted to the rank of regimental colonel.

The great object of my ambition has ever been the Horse Artillery, and having spent the best part of my life in that branch of the service, I cannot but feel most anxious not to be removed from it in this, probably, the last step of my regimental existence.

I have written a private note to Sir Hussey Vivian, expressing my wishes on the subject, but I thought it unnecessary to take up his time with a detail of any claims for service that I might bring forward; to you, therefore, I hope I may look for placing them in the most favourable light when the question comes under consideration.

Should the master-general think proper to leave me in the command of this district, along with the jacket, I shall think myself most fortunate, but the Horse Artillery is ever my first object.

Carlisle,
December 30, 1836.

My dear Lord Fitzroy,

The general expectation that there will be a brevet sometime or other prompts me to trouble you with this note, which, from the many acts of kindness I have received at your hands, I venture to hope you will forgive, on this, as you have done on so many similar occasions. Common report is so little to be relied on, that I should feel little inclined to listen to it at present; but my position in the regiment is so critical, and the importance of the step I shall receive (if a brevet should take place) to my character, as well as future comfort, is such that I cannot but feel very anxious to obtain, through your friendship, a good word in the ear of the master-general to continue me in the Horse Artillery.

Will you allow me to state my case? Supposing a brevet to promote all the colonels of 1825, I should be raised to the rank of regimental colonel, and as my great ambition has always been to continue in the Horse Artillery, with which all my early feelings are associated, I am more than ever anxious not to be separated from it, in the last step of my regimental existence, to which I hope my service in it of nearly forty years may give me some claim; but as you know all about me, I need not take up your time with any detail, for I am sure if you can with propriety put in a good word for me, I shall not want a friend.

I have written to Sir Hussey Vivian to make my wishes known to him, but I have not troubled him with any testimonials or other recommendations.

Yours faithfully,

H. D. R.

To these Sir Hew had the following answers:—

From Lord Fitzroy Somerset.

Horse Guards,
January 6, 1837.

My dear Ross,

I am happy to be able to inform you that the master-general has determined to continue your service in the Horse Artillery after your promotion.

His first answer to my application was unfavourable, but I yesterday received a note from him announcing that he had altered the arrangements he had at first in contemplation, and was consequently enabled to appoint you to the Horse Artillery. I am delighted at your success, and beg you to believe me,

Yours very faithfully,

Fitzroy Somerset.

From Sir Alexander Dickson.

Woolwich,
January 27, 1837.

My dear Ross,

I ought long ere this to have congratulated you on your continuance in the saddle, which was done with the twofold view of reward for your past services, and of retaining you in the command of the district, where it is universally admitted you have been of much public use.

The growth of Chartism made the state of the northern district again unsatisfactory. Writing to Sir Alexander Dickson, March 13, 1839, Sir Hew Ross says:—

I wish I could give a better account of this part of the country, for I am sorry to say here, as well as in the neighbouring counties of Northumberland and Durham, the Chartists are arming to a considerable extent. It was long before the civil authorities either here or at Newcastle would acknowledge the fact. Now they are aware of it; but whether from dread of becoming unpopular with their former friends, or some other cause, they are taking no precautions, and even the county magistrates appear to be trusting to Providence, for they likewise are doing nothing, as it is said, because they are unwilling to make a move in the absence of any declaration on the part of government of there being a necessity for it; so that if an outbreak should unfortunately take place, all will be looking to the troops for that protection which we cannot, weak as we are, afford them, and which, with proper energy and preparation, with our assistance they might have easily provided.

Our field artillery equipments at this period were on a most inefficient scale, and Sir Hew Ross's correspondence with Sir Alexander

Dickson shows that every exertion was made to put the artillery of the northern district in as efficient a state as the means allowed would permit. The main resort was to be the hire of post horses; Sir Alexander Dickson pointing out, in speaking of post horses for two light 6-prs. in reserve at Chester, that when once serviceable horses were procured, "it would be a great object to retain them at a daily hire when in movement, or in readiness for moving, after first marching." In two of his letters —March 18th and 26th, 1839—Sir Alexander Dickson gives the following instructions as to the employment of rockets, a rocket carriage having been supplied to each troop of Horse Artillery:—

I have in general terms to state my opinion that Horse Artillery are alone suitable to make use of rockets under the circumstances that may now arise, as the most advantageous mode of employing them when the ground is favourable would be in skirmishing order, so that the men engaged could remount and rapidly retire when pressed, or after they had fired their rockets; at the same time, when the ground is intersected by hedges and walls, the tubes would then have to be used. With this view Major Arbuthnot should be made to understand that when rockets are to be used, he should assign one of his mounted gun detachments, with two dismounted gunners on the rocket carriage, as a temporary measure; and more effectually to execute this, he should have all the articles required to advance in skirmishing order.

With regard to the question he has put to you as to the employment of rockets—*viz.*, 'On what occasions it would be advisable to use the rockets in case of the troops being called out in aid of the civil power, and whether he ought to take the two guns or one of the rocket section;' in answer I have to state that when the troop is called out in aid of the civil power, he should move with his two guns and rocket equipment, according to circumstances; and as to the employment of rockets, and what occasion, I have to observe that where the locality is suitable, and the necessity of the case should require the guns to be employed, the same necessity would render justifiable the employment of rockets. I have to add that whichever carriage is not brought into play would remain in reserve with the troops. The fact is, you quite concur with me in opinion on this.

A note dated August 12, 1839, from his old commanding officer, Lord Strafford, shows the value set at this period on Sir Hew Ross's judgment in the management of the civil force of the district:—

Dear Sir Hew Ross,

I had a conversation with Lord John Russell, in which, among other questions, he asked if I knew you. I told him that I had sent you some years since to your present command, and that he might place implicit confidence in you, to which remark he entirely assented. He said that he had unpleasant accounts from Cockermouth, or Whitehaven (I forget which), and wished I could ascertain from you whether what he had done there met with your views and concurrence.

This is of course a private communication. Hoping it will find you in good health,

I remain,

Very truly yours,

Strafford.

The outbreak of the Chartists at Monmouth, and the apprehension and trial of Frost, occurred in this year. The late Sir James Graham of Netherby was a neighbour of Sir Hew Ross's in Cumberland, and the following extracts from letters preserved by Sir Hew among his correspondence will be read with interest as showing the opinions on the state of affairs held by one of the most practical statesmen of his day:—

Private and Confidential.

Netherby,
August 10, 1839.

My dear Sir Hew,

On Wednesday last, before leaving London, I had a conversation with Lord John Russell on the state of affairs in this county. He told me that the Mayor of Carlisle had informed you *privately* that in the event of tumult no reliance was to be placed in the civil force within the city, and that the sole dependence must rest on the military for the preservation of the public peace. He asked me what I thought on the subject; I answered that I believed the statement, inasmuch as the Chartists had been sworn in as special constables, the police was insufficient, the aldermen and council violent Radicals, and the town hall had been lent by the authorities of the city for a Chartist meeting no later than last autumn.

We then talked of the neighbourhood of Carlisle, of Dalston, of Wigton, and Cockermouth, and he told me that you did not like to detach small bodies of your troops, especially since it was necessary to billet them among the inhabitants.

I then offered to him some suggestions for his Constabulary Bill, now in progress, which he has adopted, and told him that as soon as it had passed I would confer with Lord Lonsdale and some of my brother magistrates, as well as with you, for the purpose of endeavouring to bring the measure into operation in Cumberland as soon as it became law. After this conversation with Lord John Russell I saw the Duke of Wellington, to whom I communicated what had passed. He said you were quite right in being unwilling to consent to the billeting of your men. In all cases, without regard to expense, he said *entire* houses—public-houses if none other could be obtained—should be occupied by the soldiers, with barrack rules and discipline established, and, if possible, an officer in each house; and he said, if this were attended to, fifty soldiers well in hand and under good discipline could 'take care of themselves' in any town with not more than 5000 inhabitants.

I talked over the Constabulary Bill with him, and he is prepared to improve the measure in the Lords, and if possible to engraft on it a provision which may make the pensioners available in case of a serious disturbance—at once removing them out of harm's way, and rendering their military experience safe and serviceable. He strongly recommends, if we adopt the bill in Cumberland, that we should apply to Colonel Rowan for a good chief constable, who would naturally be a half-pay officer of the good old sort; and he was kind enough to say that I might write to him from time to time, and he would give me his opinion.

My first step is to report myself to you, and to say that I am ready to the utmost of my power to assist in the maintenance of the public peace; and we are most fortunate in having au officer of your character and experience on the spot, with whom we may co-operate.

An apprehension is very general in the highest quarters that something serious may be expected on Monday next. I intend to go to the moors in Bewcastle; but if you should want me, you may command my services at all times.

   I am, dear Sir Hew,
     Yours very truly,

          J. R. G. Graham.

I have sent you the Constabulary Bill, as amended by Lord John, in conformity with my suggestions. It will go to the House of Lords very much as it is, but in the House of Lords I expect it to be improved by the duke. I have no other copy, please therefore to return it, with any suggestions which may occur to you.

Netherby,
December 6, 1839.

My dear Sir Hew,

I have received this evening the enclosed letter from Mr. ——. It contains some information which appears to me important, and which the government ought to possess, with the view of tracing the alleged intercourse between Paris and London. I have informed Mr. —— that I have confided his letter to you, with a request that you will not allow his name to be used, and that you will return the letter itself to me.

I place great reliance on Mr. ——'s accuracy, but if you repeat the information contained in his letter, his name must not go further than between you and me. I have advised him to communicate directly with Lord Lonsdale, who, as Lord Lieutenant, is the proper channel of intercourse with the civil authorities.

It is right that the military authorities also should have information, and to save time I have thought it best to send you the letter. The preaching in Dalston on Sunday ought not to be neglected, and some-one should attend to take down the words spoken by ——. You of course will exercise your discretion in the use, if any, which you may think fit to make of this report; but at all events I rely on your caution that Mr. ——'s name may not transpire, for I fear, if it were known that he had given the information, his life and properly would not be safe. I write in haste, and hope you will pardon me for thus venturing to trouble you. I am always, with sincere regard, my dear Sir Hew,

Very truly yours,

J. R. G. Graham.

The following was the enclosure referred to:—

December 6, 1839.

Sir,

I beg leave to address you on a subject in which I think you will feel some anxiety. I mean the present agitation of the Chartists, which, if we may judge from symptoms, is of fearful import. You may perhaps have seen in the newspapers that there is a widely-spread system going on, not only throughout England and Wales, but that Chartism even extends into France. What I have now to state I think in some respect proves this to be the case.

The Chartist delegate —— was at —— on Saturday last, and gave a speech to his followers, which from information I obtained was to the following; purport:—He told them 'that Chartism was established from London to Paris;' that when he was in London, there were *six* young Frenchmen employed to manage the correspondence, two of whom resided in France (in Paris), two in London, in the same house as himself, and two are employed in going between the Chartists in London and the Chartists in Paris, to manage the correspondence.

He said 'there would soon be such a light burning in Paris as would light Louis Philippe's palace without the aid of gas.' He told the Chartists here 'to take care of their arms, as he did not know how soon they might be wanted to march. They were to be *always* ready.' They replied, they were ready now. He said they would soon be wanted, and he would lead them on, and place himself in the front of danger. He had seen two revolutions—one in France and one in Greece—he was present in both, and he hoped before he died to be in another—in England. (Great cheering.)

In the meantime, they were to keep up the contributions, as they could not collect when called on to march. He told them if they looked around them, they would see *plenty* among their wealthy neighbours. He said, 'I do not tell you to take it, but if you love your wives and children, you must not let them starve. You must dust the coats of your oppressors.'

These are a few of his expressions. I could give many more, but they would not be so significant. He denounced the Church, calling it the House of Mammon, and said that he would come back on Sunday, the 8th, and give them two political sermons, and he doubted not he would find very appropriate texts.

I understand he is to give the sermons as promised, and I should suppose there will be an immense concourse of people. He is to preach in the marketplace, in the open air; he intends, he says, to give lectures in every town and considerable village in the county, that he may see his strength.

I would beg to suggest that the magistrates ought to appoint, at the county expense, police officers to attend these meetings openly to obtain evidence, and to see who it is who attend them.

They, the Chartists, have besides these meetings secret committees, who have their watchwords and passes.

Stonehouse,
December 7, 1839.

My dear Sir James,

I have sent to Sir Charles Napier a copy of the three first pages of Mr. ——'s letter, but without naming him or you; neither have I in it given the name of the place, to prevent all suspicion of the writer, should the general think proper to forward it to the Home Office, when it might chance to find its way back to Carlisle. I have, however, in a confidential note, told him it refers to ——.

On the first perusal of your note, I was more than half inclined to endeavour to see, or at any rate to write to the mayor, or some other magistrate, on the subject of it; but recollecting the conversation I had with Mr. —— (of which I gave you an account), I felt that it might be considered an officious and uncalled-for interference on my part with the civil authorities, especially as I was told the other day by Lord Wallace and Major Maclean that Mr. Fawcett (who they met at Miss C.'s) had assured them that he and his colleagues have a *secret* but constant watch on, and are perfectly acquainted with, all his doings and sayings, adding that they think it prudent to affect ignorance, that the Chartists may not suspect they are watched or have informers amongst them.

The only doubt that remains is, as to whether the borough magistrates may think proper to trouble themselves with what goes on out of their own jurisdiction. If they do not it is pretty clear that nobody else will, and —— may play what pranks he thinks fit without molestation; indeed, for my part, even if it became me (acting only as a soldier) to interfere, I know not to whom I ought to address myself, Mr. —— is the only magistrate resident near ——. I believe he is not in the county at present, nor do I know that he would take any interest in the matter if he was.

Having had no communication from any of the magistrates at or around Carlisle regarding the state of its population, or the likelihood of their requiring aid from me, I must await their pleasure. All that becomes me in regard to them I have done, by expressing my readiness at all times to co-operate with them in measures to preserve the peace; were I to do more I might be thought an alarmist, without doing any good.

I hope, my dear Sir James, I need not say that I shall always be thankful to you for any information that may come to your knowledge. It may enable me to keep Sir C. Napier alive to the real state of this part of his district, and myself prepared for coming events, which I fear too many do not expect, or expecting, are afraid to look at or try to avert. I hope —— will make a similar communication to the lord lieutenant; it cannot reach the ear of Lord Normanby in too impressive a form. I return the letter, and remain,

Yours most truly

H. D. Ross.

I should not omit to mention that a great part of what is contained in Mr. ——'s letter relating to ——'s speech was mentioned to me in Carlisle some days ago, and both the bishop and Mr. Fletcher are aware of it, and of his intended sermons today; but the intercourse between Paris and London is quite new to me.

Sir James Graham again writes:—

Netherby,
December 18, 1839.

I am persuaded that the danger has by no means ceased; it will only begin to be urgent when the trials at Monmouth are in progress. Great vigilance throughout the manufacturing districts will be necessary at that moment. You will observe that a delegate is holding secret meetings at Dalston.

Netherby,
December 27, 1839.

My dear Sir Hew,

I have just now received the enclosed letter, and I think it better that you should see it without delay. It is somewhat circumstantial, and certainly points to the necessity of more immediate and active precautions than the civil authorities in Carlisle are disposed to take. I shall remain in this county over next week.

Yours very truly,

J. R. G. Graham.

I have received a note this morning saying that a Dr. ——, from Newcastle, has been over yesterday, and tells them (the Chartists) that all is ready. ——, ——, and —— are all gone south, to commence there if they can. The burning is to be before the trial—it is supposed the day before the commission is opened. I have no doubt that the exciting language held out to the people by the agitators is to the purport now stated, although I do not believe they could get the Chartists to fight in Carlisle or neighbourhood.

How far they may succeed in Lancashire, Staffordshire, Warwickshire, Cheshire, and in Wales, is probably now to be seen. Should Sir

Hew Ross not know that these men have gone off with this professed intention, perhaps you may deem it of sufficient importance to again communicate with him, as you may think it would be as well that the magistrates should be put on the alert in other places. For the last month, I am informed, the Chartists have considered Carlisle and neighbourhood their headquarters.

On Monday night last, there was a private meeting in Carlisle, when harangued his confidential followers in a solemn and prophetic tone. He particularly impressed upon them the necessity of being ready at a moment's warning, *as the time was near at hand*. He said the rise would be first in the south, after which they would follow in the north. This information is from the same source as the former part of my letter, and they all correspond with ——'s first speech at Dalston.

Netherby,
December 29, 1839.

My dear Sir Hew,

I am afraid that you will think I needlessly torment you with these enclosures; but it is as well you should see the reports; and you will observe with pleasure that your active preparations already are recognised as a salutary check on their lawless proceedings. If it had not been for you and the military, this county would have been a prey to open violence long ago.

Yours very truly,

J. R. G. Graham.

When I wrote on Friday, I stated that —— had left Carlisle, after intimating to the Chartists that he was going southward. It appears, however, that he must have changed his mind suddenly, as he was only absent one or two days. Since his return he has been acting with great caution, and has not attended the meetings of the committees. He gives as his reason for changing his conduct, that his letters are intercepted, and he is left without the requisite information.

I beg further to state that an opinion prevails that the Newport prisoners will be screened by government, and that even should conviction take place there will be no execution, and that this will be done to conciliate the Chartists. The Chartists are boasting that government dare not injure 'a hair of Frost's head.' The calico printers, who make good wages, have been subscribing 3s. a week for Frost's defence, and other workpeople have also been exceeding all their former subscriptions.

Sir Henry Bouverie had been succeeded in his command of the northern district by Lieut.-General Sir Richard Jackson, and he again by Sir Charles Napier, with both of whom Sir Hew Ross maintained the same cordial relations. Early in 1840 the serious illness of Sir Alexander Dickson made it evident that he could not, even if his life was spared, long hold the offices of Deputy Adjutant-General and Director-General of Artillery, both of which he was then filling. Some of Sir Hew Ross's friends urged him to make application for the appointment of Deputy-Adjutant-General, but as the following letter shows, unsuccessfully:—

March 14, 1840.

My dear Sir Hew,

I have this morning had a note from Lord F. Somerset, in which he says:—'Ross judges very rightly, and I do not hesitate to say that he will be firm to his purpose (for I know him well), and resist the importunities of friends who act unkindly by him in urging him to make any application. I should be very, very sorry if any. officer were to apply for our valued friend's appointment during his life, but I should indeed regret it deeply if anyone who had served with him and knew his merits were to pursue that course.' I knew that your own opinion and your own feelings were correct, but you may like to know that Lord F. agrees with them.

Yours ever,

E. J. Bridges.

In a previous letter, Feb. 21, 1840, Major Bridges mentions that Sir Hussey Vivian had told him in confidence that he thought of Sir Hew Ross as Director-General.

Sir Alexander Dickson's state having become hopeless, Sir Hew Ross received the following letter from the Master-General of the Ordnance, the late Lord Vivian, then Sir Hussey Vivian:—

My dear Sir Hew,

You will no doubt have heard of Sir A. Dickson's illness. I am grieved to say Captain Burnaby has this instant informed me his death is hourly expected. His loss to the corps as well as to me will in deed be a severe one. In looking for a successor to this admirable and excellent man as Deputy-Adjutant-General, your high character and distinguished service at once point you out to me as the person most proper to be selected. I trust, therefore, in offering you the appointment I shall in reply have the satisfaction of learning you are prepared to accept an office so responsible and so honourable. I will thank you to send your answer under cover to Colonel Maberly, at the General Post Office. I shall then get it on Sunday. Write *immediate* on the cover, and beg it may be sent to me. In great haste, ever my dear Sir Hew,

Very faithfully yours,

Hussey Vivian.

Ordnance Office,
April 17, 1840.
Half-past five p.m.

To this Sir Hew gave the following reply:—

Carlisle,
April 19, 1840.

My dear Sir Hussey,

I am much gratified by your kindness in offering to place me in the honourable and responsible office held by my lamented friend Sir A. Dickson. I am well aware of the difficulty that (coming after him) must attend the fulfilment of its duties, and were it not for the confidence with which you have honoured me, I should feel great distrust of my own powers. Being deficient in the experience so requisite to the proper discharge of official duties, I must throw myself on your indulgence, only assuring you that my best efforts shall not be wanting to give you satisfaction.

A few days later, Sir Hew Ross received the following warm-hearted and characteristic letter from Sir Charles Napier, which forms a fit conclusion for this account of the portion of his service passed in the northern district:—

Chester,
April 23, 1840.

My dear Ross,

I am exceedingly sorry to hear so hopeless an account of one who, among the soldiers of his day, shone with marked brilliance; and in what age did war produce men more hardy or more brave? England had before beaten France, but when was France what she was when Wellington overthrew her armies? If there is ought to boast of in military renown it belongs to the army of Wellington; and surely the leader of that terrible artillery which thundered through those great battles cannot die and be forgotten like an ordinary man! I hope England will not let him pass away unnoticed.

His funeral ought to be a public one, and on his tomb should be inscribed— *'He led the artillery of Wellington.'* A greater epitaph could scarcely be written except for the chief himself! The men who fought in Spain drop fast. The youngest of them must now begin to think of folding his cloak around him and falling decently. The immortality which Wellington cast over us like a mantle of light will long endure, but our bodies are becoming separate things; and more is the pity, for of all things being old is the most disagreeable, at least I find it so.

I hope you may succeed to your friend. I know of no man more worthy, none who followed him better in the field, none more like him than yourself. You say nothing of this to me, but I feel too well assured of the opinion of the *old army* not to know on whom its eyes will be cast. I wish you may *not* come back to this district, but your own advantage can alone make up to me for losing you. *Adieu,* my dear Sir Hew, and believe me that the reminiscence of former times and a renewed acquaintance have left few more sincerely yours than

C. J. Napier.

Sir Hew Ross filled the office of Deputy-Adjutant-General from the date of Sir Alexander Dickson's death to the commencement of the Crimean war, when he was appointed Lieut.-General of the Ordnance, on the Master-General, the late Lord Raglan, leaving England for the command of the army in the East.

The establishment of the Royal Artillery at the date of his appointment as Deputy-Adjutant-General (12th April, 1840), was 537 officers and 7190 men. A battery of Horse Artillery in England had 2 guns, 35 horses, and no wagons; a 9-pr. field battery, 4 guns, 4 wagons, and 44 horses. Whether as regards establishments or appliances of instruction, there were few points not requiring attention to secure the maintenance of the artillery service on an efficient scale suited to the requirements of the day.

The obstacle to improvement was its cost. An increase of 53 officers and 1441 men was procured in 1846; 4 officers and 1200 men in 1847; and 100 officers and 1354 men in 1848; but it was not till after this date, and when a full enquiry had been made into the state of our military departments by a Select Committee of the House of Commons, of which the present Duke of Somerset was chairman, that a liberal course was commenced with regard to establishments of horses and to the provision of means of instruction. So late as the 14th April, 1848, Sir Hew Ross writes :—

I intend to see the master-general tomorrow, but I fear there is no chance of his—or rather the Treasury—consenting to the addition of a horse to our meagre establishment. . . . Weedon has 19 horses, but you are under a mistake with regard to Manchester; there are only 16 horses there, although there are no less than two 6-prs. and two 24-pr. howitzers, the requisite number of horses being, when necessary, made up with *posters.* It is a sad system; but *poor England,* I suppose, can afford no better.

The events of the year 1848 led to a larger army expenditure, and our Horse Artillery and field battery establishments were gradually placed on a more efficient footing during the remainder of Sir Hew Ross's term of office, previous to the Crimean War. Many improvements were also made in the means of instruction, both for officers and men. The Royal Artillery Institution, which had been established in 1838 on a small scale, by the exertions of Major-Generals Wilmot and Lefroy, then subalterns, supported by Sir Alexander Dickson, was removed in 1853, through the exertions of Major-General Wilmot and with the support of Sir Hew Ross, to its present building, and placed on a more efficient footing, which has since enabled it to play an important part in the professional instruction of the officers.

An officer was appointed at Woolwich in the year 1850 as instructor of young officers of the Royal Artillery on first joining the service, and his appointment has since led to the gradual establishment of a Senior Department of Artillery Studies for officers of older standing.

A system introduced in the early days of Sir Hugh Ross's tenure of office of allowing officers at Woolwich to be taken off the garrison duties to attend a course of voluntary instruction in one of the Royal Arsenal departments, was extended, and led to the establishment of classes of instruction for officers and non-commissioned officers under a captain instructor in each department.

A serious deficiency in connection with the instruction of the Royal Artillery had been the want of a good practice range at Woolwich, and after long perseverance an improved practice range was at last procured in the Woolwich marshes. Objections raised to the use of the sands at Sandwich for experimental practice, led also, about the year 1852, to the formation of a small detached artillery station at Shoeburyness, which grew very quickly into the well organised School of Gunnery which now exists at that place.

The first order given in 1854, for an artillery force for the East found the Royal Artillery increased in numbers and efficiency as compared with its state in 1848, but on a small scale both of men and horses for a war of any magnitude. None of the Horse Artillery or field batteries were on a war establishment, and, in the absence of reserves, they had to be made up by means of volunteers and drafts of horses from batteries lower on the rollster for foreign service, several of which had to be afterwards sent to the seat of war. Each battery was, however, made up as required, and notwithstanding the thirty-nine years of peace and of reduced establishments which had elapsed since Sir Hew Ross had closed his own active service at the Battle of Waterloo, he had the satisfaction of seeing every battery and every portion of a battery shipped from England sent to its destination complete in itself, and in a high state of efficiency, equal to that of any artillery of that day.

Sir Hew Ross was appointed Lieut.-General of the Ordnance on the 2nd May, 1854, and carried on the duties of the master-general till the 22nd May, 1855, when the arrangements of the government for amalgamating the War and Ordnance Offices were completed, and the appointments of the master-general and other members of the Board of Ordnance were abolished. He was then placed on the staff of the commander-in-chief as Adjutant-General of Artillery at the Horse Guards, and continued in that office till the 1st April, 1858, when he retired from the active duties of the profession, after a career of 63 years of uninterrupted employment with his own arm of the service.

The confidence reposed in his judgment by the master-general under whom he served and by His Royal Highness the commander-in-chief, and the friendly and cordial relations which he maintained with a large proportion of the best officers of the Royal Artillery, acted most advantageously for the public service. His early service and his own soldierlike character had given him a high standard of efficiency, and his success in maintaining this standard in the Royal Artillery at large during his term of office, with an increase in the strength of the corps in the interval of about 350 officers and 14,000 men, was shown by the high praise uniformly given to the officers and men by the officers under whom they were serving, and the liberal rewards in promotions and other honours awarded to the officers by Her Majesty on all occasions of service.

Sir Hew Ross was created a Grand Cross of the Bath on the 19th July, 1855, and a Field-Marshal of the army on the 1st January, 1868. A public dinner was given to him and to Field-Marshal Sir John Burgoyne, Bart., G.C.B., by the officers of the Royal Artillery and Royal Engineers on the 9th March, 1868, at Willis's Rooms, at which His Royal Highness the Duke of Cambridge presided as colonel of the two corps. He was also appointed Lieut.-Governor of Chelsea Hospital in August of the same year.

He resided in London after quitting active employment, spending usually some months of the summer and autumn in the country, which his active habits enabled him thoroughly to enjoy to within a short period of his death.

He died on the 10th December, 1868, after a few days' suffering from a complaint to which he had been long subject, and which had frequently caused him an amount of suffering which few would have thought, on seeing his active walk, that he could have passed through.

The following order, issued by His Royal Highness the Commander-in-Chief, on Sir Hew Ross's retirement from active employment fitly closes this memoir of his services:—

General Order.

Horse Guards, S.W.,
April 1, 1858.

Her Majesty's Government, on the re-organisation of the general staff of the army, has deemed it expedient to abolish the appointment of Adjutant-General of Royal Artillery, held by General Sir Hew Dalrymple Ross, G.C.B.

His Royal Highness, the General Commanding-in-Chief, in losing the assistance of this distinguished officer, desires to record his sense of Sir Hew's valuable services.

For more than 63 years Sir Hew Ross has been engaged in the active duties of his profession, and he has been rewarded with the highest honours to which officers aspire.

As captain of Horse Artillery, he commanded the famous "Chestnut Troop," whose exploits while attached to the Light Division throughout the whole of the Peninsular war and at Waterloo, are so well known to the army.

In the year 1840 he was promoted to Deputy-Adjutant-General of Artillery; he subsequently became Lieut.-General of the Ordnance, and on the amalgamation of the Ordnance with the War Department, was appointed Adjutant-General of the Royal Artillery.

In every department he was famed for a steady application to the duties of his office, and for devotion to that branch of the service of which he was so conspicuous an ornament.

In war he attained great reputation, and he maintained it to the last.

By order of His Royal Highness

The General Commanding-in-Chief,

G. A. Wetherall,

Adjutant-General. Record of Services of Field-Marshal Sir Hew D. Ross,
G. C. B.

Obtained commission as 2nd Lieut. in the Royal Artillery in March, 1795. Served at Gibraltar and in Great Britain and Ireland (the latter during the rebellion) till June 1809, when proceeded to Lisbon with a troop of Horse Artillery, which he commanded throughout the campaigns in the Peninsula and at Waterloo, returning a Knight Commander of the Bath and with the brevet rank of Lieut.-Colonel.

From 1815 was employed in Great Britain and Ireland, still in command of his troop, and on promotion to regimental Lieut.-Colonelcy was appointed in 1825 Commanding Officer of Artillery in the Northern District, and subsequently during the disturbances (under the General commanding), was entrusted with the command of the troops in the four northern counties of the district.

Removed from this to be Deputy-Adjutant-General of Artillery in April, 1840, and appointed Lieut.-General of the Ordnance on May 2, 1854.

Appointed Adjutant-General of Artillery May 22, 1855, which office was abolished April 1, 1858.

Appointed Lieut.-Governor of Chelsea Hospital, August 3, 1868.

2nd Lieut., R.A.	March 6, 1795	Lieut.-General	Nov. 11, 1851.
1st Lieut., R.H.A.	May 10, 1796.	Col.-Commandant, R.H.A.	Aug. 11, 1852
Capt.-Lieut., R.A.	Sept. 1, 1803.	General	Nov. 28, 1854.
Adjutant 5th Battalion, R.A.	Sept. 12, —	Field-Marshal	Jan. 1, 1868
2nd Captain, R.A.	July 19, 1804.		
Captain, R.H.A.	July 24, 1806.		
Brevet Major	Dec. 31, 1811.		
Brevet Lieut.-Colonel	June 21, 1813.		
Lieut.-Colonel, R.H.A.	July 29, 1825.		
Brevet Colonel	July 22, 1830.		
Colonel, R.H.A.	Jan. 10, 1837.		
Major-General	Nov. 23, 1841.		
Col.-Commandant 12th Batt.	Nov. 1, 1848.		

Knight Commander of the Bath for service in
the Peninsula.

Knight of the Tower and Sword, for do.

2nd Class St. Anne of Russia, for Waterloo.

Knight Grand Cross of the Bath, July 19, 1855.

Medals for Busaco, Salamanca, Badajoz, Vittoria,
Nivelle, Nive, Waterloo, silver war medal with
three clasps for Fuentes d'Onor, Ciudad
Rodrigo, and Pyrenees.

Services in the Field.

Action in front of Alameda	July 20, 1810.	Affair of San Munoz on retreat from Madrid	Nov. 17, 1812.
Action of the Coa	July 24, —	Affair near Burgos advancing to Vittoria	June 12, 1813.
Battle of Busaco	Sept. 27, —	Affair near San Milan and Oseva	June 18, —
Actions of Pombal and Redinha, Mar. 11 & 12, 1811.		Battle of Vittoria	June 21, —
(Slightly wounded in shoulder).		Daily affairs with the French, June 22 to 27, —	
Action of Casal Nova and Foz d'Oronces Mar. 13, 14, & 15, —		Battle of the Pyrenees July 26 to 30, —	
(Slightly wounded in the leg).		Heights of San Marcial near Irun	Aug. 31, —
Action of Sabugal	April 3, —	Passage of the Bidassoa	Oct. 7, —
Battle of Fuentes d'Onor	May 5, —	Battle of the Nivelle	Nov. 10, —
Action of Aldea Ponte	Sept. 27, —	Passage of the Nive	Dec. 9, —
Siege of Ciudad Rodrigo	Jan. 19, 1812.	Battle of St. Pierre near Bayonne	Dec. 13, —
Siege of Badajoz	April 6, —	(Horse killed under him).	
(Dangerously wounded in the head).		Battle of Waterloo June 17 & 18, 1815.	
Capture of Forts at Salamanca	June 27, —	(Lost 2 horses killed under him and 1 wounded).	
Action of Castrajon	July 17, —	Capture of Paris.	
Affairs at Canazal on the Juraina	July 19, —		
Battle of Salamanca	July 22, —		
Capture of Madrid and Retiro, Aug. 12 & 14, —			

Appendix

THE CHRISTENING OF THE CHESTNUT TROOP
By Francis Duncan

In the year 1798, an expedition was ordered from England, with a view to the destruction of the basin, gates, and sluices of the Bruges Canal, and the consequent injury to the internal navigation between Holland, Flanders, and France. The prevention of a meditated invasion of England by the French would, it was hoped, by this means also be ensured. The naval part of the expedition was under the control of Captain Home Popham, while the military force was commanded by General Sir Eyre Coote. Eight companies of the Guards, the 11th Regiment, and the flank companies of the 23rd and 49th Regiments, constituted the Infantry employed; and the artillery consisted of two companies attached to a battery of four 6-pounders and three light howitzers. (D.A. Gen.'s correspondence.)

The artillery officers were Captain W. H. Walker (in command), Captain—afterwards Sir Wiltshire—Wilson, Captain C. Godfrey, Lieutenants Simpson, Hughes, Ilbert, and Holcroft. The guns were carried in different vessels, and landed near Ostend. On the 19th May, at daybreak, the troops disembarked, and commenced destroying the works. In a few hours they undid the labour of five years, besides burning a number of transports, which had been collected for the conveyance of French regiments to England; but this was not effected without considerable loss. When, however, the English force attempted to reembark, it was found to be impossible, owing to the high wind which prevailed and the heavy sea.

It was therefore found necessary, after going through the empty form of summoning the citadel, to encamp for the night on the sands. The English were attacked at daybreak by the enemy in overwhelming numbers; and after a severe action, in which Sir Eyre Coote was wounded, the whole force was compelled to surrender. The conduct of the artillery was worthy of their comrades in the battle; and their commander, Captain Walker, received wounds from which he died. Of the rest the following official mention was made:—

> Captains Wilson and Godfrey, and Lieutenants Simpson, Hughes, and Holcroft, all of the same distinguished corps, after having done everything men could do, spiked their guns and threw them over the banks at the moment the enemy was possessing himself of them. The latter gentleman, Lieutenant Holcroft, when all his men were wounded except one, remained at his gun, doing duty with it to the best of his ability. (*London Gazette*, 21 July, 1798.)

From subsequent official correspondence (D. A. Gen. R.A., to Lieut.-Gen. of the Ordnance, 14 Nov., 1798), we learn that the following officers were permitted, with their soldier-servants, to return to England on parole, of the *viz*., Captain Wilson, Lieutenants Simpson, Hughes, and Holcroft, Captain Godfrey remaining at Lille with the men. From a plaintive letter to the deputy-adjutant-general, written by the last-named officer, it would appear that the prisoners were in a very sorry plight; for he implored an advance of pay for all, as they "wanted almost everything sorely."

Next year an expedition on a larger scale took place, although not much more fortunate. It has an especial interest to the artilleryman, as being the first expedition in which a general officer of artillery was considered necessary with the force, on account of the large proportion present belonging to that arm. General Pattison, who had held a command in America, did so as an *army*, not as an *artillery* general; and General Phillips, who also commanded in that war, was merely a regimental field officer, with army rank as general. The expedition to the Helder, in 1799, had a contingent of artillery, consisting of one troop of horse artillery, and eight companies of marching artillery, as they were termed.

The troop was A, or the Chestnut Troop, commanded by Major Judgson; and although part of it had taken a share in the suppression of the Irish rebellion, this was the first occasion on which any portion of the Royal Horse Artillery proceeded on *foreign* active service; and, as will appear, the troop had rather a rough *baptême de feu*. General Farrington was selected for the command of artillery, receiving the following letter from the deputy adjutant-general, on the 8th August, 1799:—

In conversation yesterday with Lord Howe, he observed that if the expedition now embarked was to be followed by the troops and artillery ordered to be in preparation, he should consider it necessary for them to be accompanied by not only an artillery officer of experience and abilities, but by one high in rank in the corps; and under that idea I was desired to address myself to you, to know if your health would admit of his proposing you to the commander-in-chief for the command of the whole....

The offer was eagerly accepted by the general, and his appointment was confirmed. He selected Captain—afterwards Sir William—Robe as his brigade-major, and Captain Maclean as his *aide-de-camp*.

The expedition was in two divisions: the first, under Sir Ralph Abercromby, going from Southampton, while the second, and main division, was being assembled in Kent. When united, the command-in-chief was to be assumed by the Duke of York. Sir R. Abercromby applied for Lieut. Colonel—afterwards Sir Francis—Whitworth to command the wrtillery of his division, and his request was complied. with. (MS Returns to the Board of Ordnance.) The following was the strength of General Abercromby's artillery, *viz.*: 1 field officer, 6 captains, 13 subalterns, 2 surgeons, 40 non-commissioned officers, 371 gunners, and 6 drummers. There were also present with him, belonging to the Driver Corps, 1 subaltern, 3 quartermaster commissaries, 15 non-commissioned officers, 152 drivers, 5 artificers, and 200 horses.

The main artillery force, under General Farrington, which followed that just given, was of considerable strength, (D.A. Gen.'s correspondence,) including, besides Major Judgson's troop, Lieut.-Colonels Smith and Trotter, 9 captains, 14 subalterns, 1 surgeon, 43 non-commissioned officers, 412 gunners, and 8 drummers, besides a detachment of the Driver Corps, consisting of 1 captain, 4 quartermaster-commissaries, 12 non-commissioned officers, 166 drivers, 9 artificers, and 400 horses. The strength of Major Judgson's troop was as follows: 2 captains, 3 subalterns, 1 surgeon, 16 non-commissioned officers, 97 gunners, 58 drivers, 7 artificers, and 1 trumpeter; making a total of 185, besides 191 horses.

★★★★★★

The detail of the Chestnut Troop, as it actually embarked, *exclusive of officers, officers' horses, and the attached men from the Driver*

Corps, included above was as follows:—

State of a Troop of Horse Artillery as they embarked for Holland in 1799.

		Staff-Serjeants.	Serjeants.	Corporals.	Bombardiers.	Gunners.		Drivers.	Artificers and Trumpeters.	Horses.		
						Mounted.	Dismounted.			Riding.	Draught.	Total.
4	Two 12-pounders and two ammunition waggons . . .	..	1	1	2	12	8	10	..	16	20	36
4	Two Royal howitzers and two ammunition waggons . .	..	1	1	2	12	8	8	..	16	16	32
6	Three 6-pounders and three ammunition waggons . .	..	1	1	2	20	12	12	..	24	24	48
1	One field-officer's waggon .	..	..	..	..	..	..	2	..	..	4	4
4	Four tilted baggage waggons .	..	..	..	..	..	..	8	..	..	16	16
2	Two forges	..	..	..	..	..	..	4	..	..	8	8
	Staff-serjeants	2	..	..	..	..	..	..	..	2	..	2
	Artificers and trumpeters, as per margin*	..	..	..	..	..	..	..	8	6	..	6
	Officers' servants	..	..	..	..	..	6	1	..	..	..	..
3	Spare limbers, with ammunition	..	..	..	..	..	..	3	..	..	6	6
	Number required	2	3	3	6	44	34	48	8	64	94	158
	Spare	..	..	..	..	4	4	6	..	6	10	16
24	Total of one troop . .	2	3	3	6	48	38	54	8	70	104	174

* N.B. Artificers and trumpeters for seven guns :—3 farriers—2 mounted, 1 dismounted. 1 carriage smith mounted. 2 collar-makers, 1 mounted, 1 dismounted. 1 wheeler mounted. 1 trumpeter mounted.

★★★★★★

A second troop of Horse Artillery was put under orders, but did not embark, (Captain Scott's troop, later A Battery, B Brigade); and of a further detachment of the Driver Corps, which was held in readiness, consisting of 226 men and 400 horses, about one-half ultimately went, if not more.

The whole artillery force which it was at first intended should be sent—including the Driver-Corps auxiliaries—amounted to 1857 officers and men and 1344 horses; and of this number certainly 1600 men and 1000 horses accompanied the expedition. Among the names of officers not yet mentioned, who accompanied the army to the Helder, the letters of the period include the following: Brevet Lieut.-Colonel Terrot, Major Lewis, Captain Mudge, Captain—afterwards Sir Augustus—Frazer, Captain Riou, Captain Nicholls, Captain Ramsey, Captain-Lieutenant Geary, Lieutenant Knox, Lieutenant Morrison, and Assistant-Surgeon Jameson.

From other sources we learn that two officers, who subsequently attained great distinction in the corps, were of also present—Sir E. C. Whinyates and Sir John Michell—both officers being then 2nd

Lieutenants. (*Memoir* Sir E. C. Whinyates.) Lieutenants Simpson and Eligée are also known to have been present, (Kane's List), from the fact that both were among the wounded in the actions which took place. (Browne's *England's Artillerymen.*) The reason why uncertainty prevails as to the regimental details of the artillery force on this expedition will appear at the end of this section.

It will be readily understood that so large a force was not collected without difficulty. But of the extent of the labour involved no one can adequately judge who has not had access to the official letter-books of the time. The expedition to the Helder proved at once the necessity of a head-quarters staff for the Royal Artillery, and the capacity of the man who had been selected as the first deputy-adjutant-general of the corps. The later campaigns, in whose organisation Sir John Macleod had so large a share, were undoubtedly on a grander scale; but it is questionable whether his zeal, tact, and activity were ever so prominent, as in the arrangements for this unfortunate expedition to Holland. He did everything, and made a point of knowing everything, himself: he gave himself no rest until he had accomplished his purpose; nor yet did the amount of his official labours interfere with the courtesy to all ranks for which he was so remarkable.

A private letter of friendly notice always preceded the order for movement, where such intimation could be given without detriment to the service; no unnecessary mystery attended his actions: he was almost laboriously anxious to meet the convenience of all concerned, and evinced in his letters a sympathy, such as he could not have surpassed in his dealings with his own relations. His correspondence with the various commanding officers, from under whose control he had to steal detachments to bring the companies for service up to their required strength, is a masterpiece. Never for one moment leaving the line of action which necessity and the board had imposed on him, he yet seemed to consult and defer to the generals whose divisions he was. weakening, and to obtain by their consent what he really was taking by force.

If ever a wrong system, such as the old dual government of the artillery was, could be made less detestable, it was made so by Colonel Macleod's tact and courtesy. And it is better that the deformities of a military system should be laid bare in time of *peace*, than on the eve of *war*, when the almost inevitable confusion cannot afford to be increased by ill-timed revelations. An indifferent machine well-worked is better than an admirable one whose powers are paralysed by some temporary, but thorough disarrangement. It is not when breakers are ahead, that men speculate on the beauties of their engines: it is *then* that—be they what they may—they are expected to work to the utmost of their power. In the hands of Colonel Macleod, the evils of a wrong system were reduced to a *minimum*: but the system was a wrong one still.

His exertions to perfect the force which he had to organise were as admirable as were his endeavours to remove all possible friction. There have been times in our military history when the great wheel of progress and success has—after much creaking—been set in motion by the untiring exertions of unexpected leaders, or uncomplaining heroism in the ranks, instead of the labours of those on whom the organization of the armies depended. And at such times of unexpected fortune, it has generally been found that the official flies have buzzed most loudly around the revolving wheel, as if they had been the motive power. Not so with Colonel Macleod in 1799. Nothing was beneath his notice; no exertion was spared by him which could ensure the perfection, as well as the harmony, of the machine.

The same pages which reveal his consideration for individuals show also his determination to render the artillery part of the expedition unrivalled: and the difficulties in his way were very great. In the single item of horses, he found an obstacle which seemed likely to be insurmountable; for the horses did not exist in the service, and could hardly be bought. Such animals as were procured by scouring the country were in so wretched a condition that they could barely crawl in harness. So important was every day of decent rations to the sorry brutes, that to every party marching to the port of embarkation Ramsgate—Colonel Macleod sent orders to shorten the marches, and to delay going on board as long as possible— and at all hazards, "except," he wrote, "that of allowing it to be said, 'We are waiting for the Ordnance.'"

Among other evils was the monotonous cry from distant colonies—not only heard in 1799, nor by one deputy adjutant-general—of "More men from England!" Every place was drained of every available man; even the old gunners at the Tower were drafted away, and raw recruits sent in their place: but the colonial wants were not satisfied. Militia regiments, which were embodied, were also sending daily petitions for battalion guns, followed by remonstrances and strongly-worded indignation. And Colonel Macleod, in spite of his personal opinions, was obliged to strain every nerve to meet a wish, which was still supported by our military system. His *personal* opinions, it has been said—and truly: for the correspondence of the period reveals the fact that Colonel Macleod had commenced to detest the existing system of battalion guns. He dared not say openly what he thought; but from a private letter written at this time his opinion may be easily learnt. Writing of some detachments which had been collected under an officer's command, he said:—

I believe they are intended for the battalion guns of the in-fantry brigades, and I had some thoughts of drawing them to Chatham, where I would have them drilled to the duty expect-ed of them—appointing 1 non-commissioned officer and 7 gunners to each 6-pounder, and accustoming them to make use of a horse to advance, *instead of drag-rope men* a custom which weakens the battalions they are attached to without aiding the services of the artillery. For, between you and I, six men are *too few to drag guns*, and *too many to stand with ropes in their hands to be shot at.* (Letter to Colonel—afterwards Sir John—Smith.)

An incident, which occurred at this time, shows that the system of drawing lots was not confined to choice of stations or barracks at home. In a letter to the commanding officer at Newcastle—Colo-nel Lawson—Colonel Macleod, in calling for one of the companies under his command for service in the expedition, requested him to assemble the captains, and make them draw lots for the duty.

It was in August 1799 that the force sailed from England; and the student, who has realised the labours of Colonel Macleod, will also be able to conceive the feelings of relief with which he despatched, at 3 a.m. on a day at the beginning of that month, a mounted orderly, to carry the intelligence from Woolwich to the Duke of York at Deal, that the last man and horse of the Artillery had embarked. It will now be necessary to follow the expedition, merely remarking here that the casualties, which speedily occurred, rendered a fresh supply of ammu-nition and horses necessary before many weeks had passed, and that consequently Colonel Macleod had but a brief respite from his toil.

The expedition to the Helder was intended to effect two things—the capture of the Dutch fleet, which in the hands of the French was an unmistakable danger to England, and a military demonstration in Holland, which should lead to a rising against the Republican Gov-ernment. In the first of these objects the expedition succeeded; in the second it miserably failed. For an exhibition of fruitless gallantry, it has not been surpassed in the annals of the British Army. But happily, it was the closing scene in the drama of military failure, with which the last decade of the eighteenth century was surfeited. With the new century came a spirit in England's military operations, which made her campaigns by land as glorious as her successes by sea.

The wars of the nineteenth century threw into the background the share taken by our armies in the wars of the French Revolution, during the period which preceded the overthrow of the Directorate in France and the virtual assumption of the supreme power by Napoleon in the winter of 1799. But the Regimental historian has to bring even fruitless and unsuccessful wars to light again, in his search for stories of individual gallantry or for the causes of failure.

England's ally in the expedition to the Helder was Russia. It had been arranged by the two governments that the land forces should comprise a Russian contingent of 17,000 men, and an English army of 13,000. England more than fulfilled her promise; for the actual force sent by her was as much as that promised as the Russian contribution. In addition, England furnished vessels to assist in the transport of the Russian troops from the Baltic, and a powerful fleet, of more than sixty men-of-war, under Admiral Lord Duncan.

On the 21st August, 1799, the fleet and transports arrived off the mouth of the Zuyder Zee, and anchored off the Helder: but foul weather prevented a disembarkation until the 27th, a delay which gave undoubted advantage to the French and Batavian troops. The enemy was at first under the command of General Daendels, but he was almost immediately superseded by General Brune; and the army, which had at first been 10,000 strong, rose in a few weeks to nearly treble that number.

Abercromby's division was the first to land, and after a very severe engagement, in which the infantry under General Sir James Pulteney and Coote behaved most gallantly, the Dutch were driven back, and the English took possession of the Kirkduin, and the fort of the Helder. (23rd, 27th, 29th, 55th and 85th Regiments.) The artillery was not landed till after this engagement; nor was the ground favourable to the use of the Dutch artillery. The fleet was summoned to surrender: and the Dutch Admiral, conscious of a strong spirit of insubordination among his crews, ever since the appearance of the British flag, consented to deliver over his ships unconditionally; and he thus gave to the English the complete control of the Zuyder Zee.

On this taking place, the Dutch troops retired, and took up a position in front of Alkmaar, where they were joined by General Brune and 7000 French. Abercromby occupied the ground vacated by the Dutch, and strengthened it in every way possible, being resolved to await there the arrival of the Duke of York and the Russian contingent. General Brune, however, saw the advantage of an engagement before such a junction could be effected; and therefore on the 10th September he assumed the offensive, but without success—being totally defeated with a loss of 2000 men.

The artillery was of great service to Abercromby; and it was in this engagement—known as the action of Zyp—that Lieutenant Simpson was wounded. (*London Gazette*, 16 Sept. 1799.) The French resumed their old position in front of Alkmaar, which they greatly strengthened; and -confined their operations to preventing Abercromby from advancing out of the contracted space in which he was situated.

On the 12th September the Russians arrived, and on the day following the Duke of York assumed the command, and resolved on leaving the position where the army had been stationed, and on attacking the enemy with the large force now at his disposal, numbering about 35,000 men.

He divided his army into four columns: the right being under General Hermann, and composed entirely of Russians; the second, under General Dundas, consisting partly of British, and partly of Russians; the third, under Sir James Pulteney, with a large proportion of artillery and cavalry; and the fourth, under Sir Ralph Abercromby, consisting entirely of British troops; the last being intended to make a detour on the evening of the 18th September—the day before the intended battle—and to turn the enemy's right flank.

The first three columns were ordered to attack simultaneously at break of day on the 19th, moving on different named points. These arrangements, which have been somewhat severely criticised, would doubtless have succeeded, had the duke's orders been obeyed; but unfortunately the first, or Russian, column precipitated the engagement by attacking the enemy two or three hours before the other columns were ready to move, and drove the enemy out of the village of Bergen. General Brune brought up his reserve to recover his lost ground, and fell upon the Russian troops when in a state of intoxication from the excesses of which they had been guilty since the capture of the village.

A disgraceful scene followed, ending in the tumultuous flight of the Russians with the loss of many prisoners. The Duke of York accompanied the second column, but the retreat of the Russians on his right compelled him to fall back, and to send orders to the third and fourth columns to do the same. Great success had in the meantime attended the efforts of Sir James Pulteney—the Guards, 17th and 40th Regiments, having greatly distinguished themselves; but, owing to the change given to the whole plan by the mistake and misbehaviour of the first column, when night came the Allies occupied precisely the same ground as they held in the morning.

The loss to the English amounted to 500 killed and wounded, and 500 taken prisoners;—and the Russians lost 3000 men; but an equal number of the enemy had been taken prisoners by the Allies. In this engagement, known as the Battle of Bergen or Alkmaar, the loss of the Royal Artillery was as follows, (*London Gazette*, 24 Sept. 1799):—

First Lieutenant Eligée, wounded and taken prisoner;
Volunteer John Douglass, wounded;
Killed: 5 gunners; 4 gunner-drivers; and 3 additional gunners.
Wounded: 8 gunners; 6 gunner-drivers; and 4 additional gunners.
Missing: 7 gunners, and gunner-drivers.

In the interval between this engagement and the severe battle on the 2nd October—when the event occurred which gives the title to this section—both armies were employed in strengthening their positions on shore, in obtaining reinforcements, and in arranging their respective gun-boats in such a way as to obtain from them an enfilade fire, in event of attack.

The Duke of York felt the importance of making a final effort, before the season was further advanced: and his dispositions on the 2nd October were much the same as on the 19th September, except that he gave the right column to General Abercromby, whose force consisted of 8000 infantry and 1000 cavalry, with Major Judgson's troop of Horse Artillery.

The troop was partly armed with 12-pounders—a very heavy armament for Horse Artillery, and one never again used:—and it seems all the more unsuitable, when we find that the battalion guns, which were merely 6-pounders, were in one instance brigaded into a battery under Captain Frazer—presenting the anomaly in the army, on this 2nd October, of a *light* field artillery, intended for rapid movements, being armed with guns of twice the calibre of those used by what should have been the *medium* field artillery, and only required to accommodate itself to the movements of infantry. (General Farrington to D.A.G., 17 Sept. 1799.)

The second column was composed of Russian troops, under Count

Essen; the third was under General Dundas; and the fourth under Sir James Pulteney. The main interest attaches to the first column, whose duty it was to keep close to the seashore as far as Egmont-op-Zee, and thence menace the French left and rear. The other columns were to drive back the enemy's line if possible; and, at all events, so to occupy him as to prevent the left from being strengthened in such a manner as might endanger the success of the first column.

The exertions of General Dundas's brigade were marvellous, and were crowned by success; but they were almost undone by the refusal of the Russians, at a critical moment, to advance against the village of Bergen, which had been laid bare by the retreat of the enemy before the impetuosity of the English troops. This refusal was never forgotten, nor was there from that hour any harmony between the allied troops. Encouraged by the impunity allowed them, the enemy resumed the offensive; but, although unable to drive them farther back, the English succeeded, although with great loss and difficulty, in holding the ground they had taken.

The first column, under General Abercromby, reached Egmont-op-Zee without difficulty; but there it found a large force of all arms, under General Vandamme, drawn up in line of battle. The engagement which followed was prolonged and bloody. Sir Ralph was at last successful; but his advantage was short-lived, for reinforcements arrived from Alkmaar in such numbers that it required all the skill of the English general, and all the undaunted courage of his men, to prevent his left from being broken before night put an end to the engagement. It was at this time that the Chestnut Troop received its baptism of fire. By some oversight on the part of the general, or possibly owing to ignorance as to the powers of this new weapon—Horse Artillery—Major Judgson's troop had been advanced to a dangerous distance, and left with an inadequate escort.

General Vandamme observed this, and, placing himself at the head of his cavalry, swept down upon the guns. The scene which followed was an exciting one. Taken by surprise, the gunners did not loose their presence of mind, but fired into the advancing cavalry until they were in their midst; and then, with any weapons they could lay hands on, they struggled with the troopers, who, in immense numbers, surrounded them, and sabred them at their guns. According to one Browne, account, two only of the guns were carried off by the cavalry when they retired; according to another, the whole were captured. Be it as it may, the prize was not left long undisputed, for Lord Paget, placing himself at the head of the 15th Light Dragoons—later the 15th (King's) Hussars—charged the enemy's cavalry, pursuing them for over a mile; and, assisted by the explosion of one of the captive limbers, succeeded in recovering all the guns.

The story is calculated to create a friendly sympathy between the Chestnut Troop and the gallant regiment which proved so staunch a godfather to it at this its christening, and is one to be talked over by the camp-fire in days coming on. In the order which was issued after the battle, Major Judgson received special mention.

> In the severe action on this day His Royal Highness expressed his thanks to Lieutenant-Colonels Whitworth and Smith, who commanded the artillery of reserve, and to Major Judgson, of the Horse Artillery. Captain Nicholls was wounded in this action, and is since dead. (*London Gazette*, 24 Oct. 1799.)

Although the Allies had not driven the enemy back as far as they had hoped, they nevertheless occupied the ground on which the French general had taken up his position at the commencement of the battle. The loss to the British was severe, 1300 having been killed and wounded, including 100 officers.

Another attempt was made by the Allies on the 7th October to drive the enemy back, and to escape from the position in which they had been cramped since the commencement of the campaign; but, although they defeated with severe loss the troops to whom they found themselves immediately opposed, the *cordon* beyond still hopelessly surrounded them.

As there was no symptom of a popular rising in the country on their behalf, and as reinforcements were daily reaching the French, the Duke of York decided on opening negotiations with a view to the evacuation of Holland by the Allies. These were ultimately successful; and the only beneficial result of this campaign, which survived the negotiations, was the retention of the Dutch fleet by the English.

The conclusion of the artillery share in this campaign had an element of the ludicrous in it.

In the old letter-books, deposited in the Royal Artillery Record Office, is the following one, showing the pitiable way in which poor General Farrington, who had left with all the pomp and circumstance of war, returned to his home. Writing from Blackheath, (to D. A.G. Nov. 3, 1799), he says:—

After a very fatiguing voyage and journey, I am this moment arrived at my own house. Trotter, Smith, Terrott, Robe, Maclean, Lieut. Knox, and Dr. Jameson, came over passengers with me, and will be at Woolwich this night, or tomorrow morning. The want of horses keeps them back, and my anxiety of mind to arrive as early as possible led me to accept a passage in a post-chaise; but I have a melancholy tale to unfold.

The ship in which we came passengers, mistaking the entrance into Yarmouth Harbour, ran on the sands, on which she struck with such violence as, with the first shock, to unship her rudder, and stave in her bottom; but, wonderful to tell, after keeping us in a most distressed state for an hour, she passed the sands with 4 feet of water in her hold, and, by the exertion of the boats of the fleet, every soul on board was saved—about 70 in number; and in about half an hour the ship sank in 10 or 11 fathoms of water.

The cargo, such as guns, shot, and shells, may be saved; the ammunition, of course, destroyed; and *we are all reduced to our ship-dress only*; everything else lost. It has been a most providential escape, and sincerely ought we to offer up our prayers for His mercy.

I am too unwell to wait upon Lord Howe, *nor have I things to see him in*; but if you could ride over here tomorrow, I will tell you all I can respecting the embarkation of the artillery horses, &c., *for I have not a paper left*.

While sympathising with the ill-fated general, the student cannot refrain from anathematising the blundering pilot, who mistook the entrance to Yarmouth Harbour, and was thus the cause of papers being lost which would doubtless have been priceless to the compiler of a narrative of the artillery share in the campaign of 1799.

The following return of the losses of the Royal Artillery, (return dated Woolwich, 5 Dec. 1799), *exclusive* of the Driver Corps, in this campaign, was rendered by the deputy-adjutant-general to the Board of Ordnance:—

Killed, and died of their wounds	25 of all ranks.
Wounded	21 " " "
Prisoners and Missing	15 " " "
Horses sent from England	910
Received in Holland from the Com. -General's Department	200

	1110
Total.	1110
Killed, dead, and left behind	654
Returned to England	456

(Signed)   J. Macleod,
                                            D.A .-General.

LEONAUR

ALSO FROM LEONAUR
AVAILABLE IN SOFTCOVER OR HARDCOVER WITH DUST JACKET

THE FALL OF THE MOGHUL EMPIRE OF HINDUSTAN *by H. G. Keene*—By the beginning of the nineteenth century, as British and Indian armies under Lake and Wellesley dominated the scene, a little over half a century of conflict brought the Moghul Empire to its knees.

LADY SALE'S AFGHANISTAN *by Florentia Sale*—An Indomitable Victorian Lady's Account of the Retreat from Kabul During the First Afghan War.

THE CAMPAIGN OF MAGENTA AND SOLFERINO 1859 *by Harold Carmichael Wylly*—The Decisive Conflict for the Unification of Italy.

FRENCH'S CAVALRY CAMPAIGN *by J. G. Maydon*—A Special Correspondent's View of British Army Mounted Troops During the Boer War.

CAVALRY AT WATERLOO *by Sir Evelyn Wood*—British Mounted Troops During the Campaign of 1815.

THE SUBALTERN *by George Robert Gleig*—The Experiences of an Officer of the 85th Light Infantry During the Peninsular War.

NAPOLEON AT BAY, 1814 *by F. Loraine Petre*—The Campaigns to the Fall of the First Empire.

NAPOLEON AND THE CAMPAIGN OF 1806 *by Colonel Vachée*—The Napoleonic Method of Organisation and Command to the Battles of Jena & Auerstädt.

THE COMPLETE ADVENTURES IN THE CONNAUGHT RANGERS *by William Grattan*—The 88th Regiment during the Napoleonic Wars by a Serving Officer.

BUGLER AND OFFICER OF THE RIFLES *by William Green & Harry Smith*—With the 95th (Rifles) during the Peninsular & Waterloo Campaigns of the Napoleonic Wars.

NAPOLEONIC WAR STORIES *by Sir Arthur Quiller-Couch*—Tales of soldiers, spies, battles & sieges from the Peninsular & Waterloo campaingns.

CAPTAIN OF THE 95TH (RIFLES) *by Jonathan Leach*—An officer of Wellington's sharpshooters during the Peninsular, South of France and Waterloo campaigns of the Napoleonic wars.

RIFLEMAN COSTELLO *by Edward Costello*—The adventures of a soldier of the 95th (Rifles) in the Peninsular & Waterloo Campaigns of the Napoleonic wars.

LEONAUR

ALSO FROM LEONAUR
AVAILABLE IN SOFTCOVER OR HARDCOVER WITH DUST JACKET

OFFICERS & GENTLEMEN *by Peter Hawker & William Graham*—Two Accounts of British Officers During the Peninsula War: Officer of Light Dragoons by Peter Hawker & Campaign in Portugal and Spain by William Graham .

THE WALCHEREN EXPEDITION *by Anonymous*—The Experiences of a British Officer of the 81st Regt. During the Campaign in the Low Countries of 1809.

LADIES OF WATERLOO *by Charlotte A. Eaton, Magdalene de Lancey & Juana Smith*—The Experiences of Three Women During the Campaign of 1815: Waterloo Days by Charlotte A. Eaton, A Week at Waterloo by Magdalene de Lancey & Juana's Story by Juana Smith.

JOURNAL OF AN OFFICER IN THE KING'S GERMAN LEGION *by John Frederick Hering*—Recollections of Campaigning During the Napoleonic Wars.

JOURNAL OF AN ARMY SURGEON IN THE PENINSULAR WAR *by Charles Boutflower*—The Recollections of a British Army Medical Man on Campaign During the Napoleonic Wars.

ON CAMPAIGN WITH MOORE AND WELLINGTON *by Anthony Hamilton*—The Experiences of a Soldier of the 43rd Regiment During the Peninsular War.

THE ROAD TO AUSTERLITZ *by R. G. Burton*—Napoleon's Campaign of 1805.

SOLDIERS OF NAPOLEON *by A. J. Doisy De Villargennes & Arthur Chuquet*—The Experiences of the Men of the French First Empire: Under the Eagles by A. J. Doisy De Villargennes & Voices of 1812 by Arthur Chuquet .

INVASION OF FRANCE, 1814 *by F. W. O. Maycock*—The Final Battles of the Napoleonic First Empire.

LEIPZIG—A CONFLICT OF TITANS *by Frederic Shoberl*—A Personal Experience of the 'Battle of the Nations' During the Napoleonic Wars, October 14th-19th, 1813.

SLASHERS *by Charles Cadell*—The Campaigns of the 28th Regiment of Foot During the Napoleonic Wars by a Serving Officer.

BATTLE IMPERIAL *by Charles William Vane*—The Campaigns in Germany & France for the Defeat of Napoleon 1813-1814.

SWIFT & BOLD *by Gibbes Rigaud*—The 60th Rifles During the Peninsula War.